W9-CHO-892

Cruising

JOANNA & BEN HALL

Cruising

JOANNA & BEN HALL

NEW
HOLLAND

CANCELLED
WILLOUGHBY
WILLOUGHBY CITY
LIBRARY
CITY LIBRARY

Acknowledgments

Many people contributed directly or indirectly to this book, and we are extremely grateful for everyone's help and input.

Firstly, we would also like to thank our friend and unofficial agent, Patsy Rowe, for her valuable time, her incredible wisdom and her invaluable advice. Also our wonderful publisher, Fiona Shultz, for backing this book in the first place.

But this book wouldn't have been possible without the Regent Seven Seas Cruises and Crystal Cruises. We thank both cruise lines for their generosity and support of this book, especially Andrew Poulton of Regent, Mimi Weisband of Crystal, and Diane Patrick of Wiltrans Australia.

Also, there are many other people working on board ship for both cruise lines—Hotel Directors, Food and Beverage Managers, executive chefs and bartenders—all of whom helped us in some way with our on-board photo shoots, food shots, menus and other ship information. There are too many to mention by name but they know who they are and we appreciate their efforts when we have cruised.

We would also like to thank the guest chefs—Anton Mosimann, Benjamin Christie, Nobu Matsuhisa and Michel Richard—who gave us valuable input about their experiences cruising with Regent and Crystal, and also shared with us some of their amazing recipes. Thanks also to the kind people who work with them and helped to coordinate what we needed: Theresa Croll, Yukari Hirata-Elston and Mel Davis.

Finally, there is one other key person who has lived the journey of this book with us, supported our endeavours, helped to make things happen and who ultimately deserves a very special mention. He is our dear friend and favourite senior cruise director, Barry Hopkins.

Thank you all for your help and support—it won't be forgotten.

Foreword

As the travel industry grows worldwide, it's little wonder that the popularity of cruising is also surging, with more than 20 million people taking a cruise holiday each year.

An increase in the number of retirees and a healthier, wealthier population means more people are looking for holidays that offer more than a mere break from routine. There is no doubt that luxury cruising fits the bill. After all, what better way to explore the globe than from the comfort of your own private balcony on an intimately-sized, elegantly appointed ship?

Luxury cruise lines offer unparalleled service, all inclusive pricing and complete attention to detail in an uncrowded environment on ships that vary from 'yacht style' to 'all-balcony suite' vessels. They also offer a stunning array of itineraries—from voyages on the Amazon in deepest South America, to cruises through the icy waters of the Baltic. In fact, these vessels often visit places that are only accessible by water, giving passengers the true thrill of discovering a destination by sea. In most cases, luxury ships are also a destination in themselves, something that passengers can truly appreciate during languid days at sea.

Recognising the interests of their clientele, the top cruise lines offer cuisine prepared by some of the world's leading chefs and wine from the world's best vineyards. Needless to say, the service is also world class, but it's the many little things that make luxury cruising such a remarkable experience. From intimate champagne picnics on secluded beaches to lectures from some of the world's leading authorities on history and nature, luxury cruises are exceptional from the moment you board your vessel until your final disembarkation.

I hope you enjoy your journey through this book and your next voyage on the seas.

Brett Jardine

BRETT JARDINE
General Manager
International Cruise Council Australasia

Contents

Introduction

My love affair with cruising began 20 years ago on a week-long cruise of the Caribbean. I vividly remember arriving at the port of Miami and the thrill of my first glimpse of the sleek, white hull of the cruise ship which would be my home for the next seven days. It was a special feeling which grew stronger and when we finally sailed, my excitement was further fueled by the boom of the ship's horn as we pulled away from the dock, the infectious music of the steel band and the anticipation among my fellow passengers as we slipped out into the open ocean.

What followed was a memorable week of cruising, during which I visited five diverse and colourful Caribbean destinations. Some of the more exciting things I had the opportunity to do included swimming with rays in Antigua, climbing a waterfall in Jamaica, and exploring a bizarre network of underground caves in Barbados. There was also the unique experience of cruising itself, especially the times we were at sea with what felt like endless kilometres of open ocean stretching beyond the bows of the ship. It was a vacation which was ultimately relaxing, frequently eye-opening and from that first time proved to be a wonderful opportunity to make new friends.

Cruising the high seas on a ship has long been regarded as a romantic throwback to a bygone era of travel, where the salty air, open ocean and the anticipation of the next port's delights blend into a unique and memorable experience. The luxury end of the market takes this sentiment even further. As I have discovered, it's a unique opportunity to explore exotic and difficult-to-reach regions of the world in comfort and style, while being royally pampered. What's not to love about dining on gourmet cuisine and sipping on some of the world's finest wines as the dramatic landscapes of Alaska, Europe and Asia effortlessly slip by your window?

Ben's first experience of cruising was a week-long voyage through the stunning archipelago of Tahiti, on board Regent's intimate luxury ship, the Paul Gauguin. As we sailed from Papeete that night, I need not have worried if he would enjoy what lay ahead. As we stood on our private balcony with French champagne in hand, one of French Polynesia's famed sunsets began to dominate the sky with nearby Moorea as a backdrop. He was hooked. As a photographer, however, the trip proved to be both a blessing and a nightmare. At almost every turn, both on land and at sea, there was an amazing sight to see and photograph: from pristine beaches and exotic marine life, to charming villages and remote atolls. As for kaleidoscopic sunsets, let's just say we possess an impressive collection on film!

Since our first cruises, Ben and I have been lucky enough to explore many great regions of our fascinating world, a large number of them by ship. We've also enjoyed a plethora of experiences which are unique to cruising—anchoring off the remote Marquesas Islands in French Polynesia, sailing up the Saigon River in Vietnam, transiting the Panama Canal and navigating New Zealand's dramatic Milford Sound among them. Then there are the great cities we've visited from a ship, including New York, Montréal, Hong Kong, Ho Chi Minh City, Istanbul, Athens and Monte Carlo. Some of these experiences and more, are featured in this book. We hope you enjoy the voyage with us.

Joanna Hall

North America

01:
North America

The third-largest continent in the world, North America possesses virtually every type of geography and climate known to man. From east to west, and north to south, this vast landscape undulates with diversity. It's a land of dramatic coastlines, mountain ranges, deserts, the tropics, and a sub-Arctic wilderness and when it comes to cruising, North America is where two of the most popular short-season cruises take place, Canada and New England in the east, and Alaska in the west. What gives these two regions such a loyal following is easy to see once you have travelled there. Canada's unpopulated, wide open spaces truly come into their own along the magnificent St. Lawrence River, especially in the autumn months when the landscape burns with rich colour. Then there's Alaska— large, dramatic and isolated, a place where the term 'the last frontier' still applies.

Canada & New England

It's a show of epic proportions and every year towards the end of September, North America's vast forests and national parks change colour. It's nature at her most beguiling: the dazzling transformation of hardwood canopies from lush green into a brilliant explosion of scarlet, bronze and gold. Witnessing the change of season has become an obsession for countless enthusiasts. Throngs of 'leaf peepers' make the annual pilgrimage to the eastern seaboard on foot, in cars, on buses and on cruise ships in search of foliage ecstasy, which is the moment when the blazing rite of autumn is at its most colourful. The peak time for cruising in the North American autumn varies; September and October are best months, but even if Mother Nature doesn't co-operate and the foliage show is late, it's an experience that's not just for the leaf peepers. Historical cities, picture-postcard ports, deserted islands and the untouched wilderness are a part of the journey through the maritime provinces of Canada and the eastern seaboard of the United States.

MONTRÉAL

Many cruises start or end in Montréal, which is considered by many visitors to be one of the most 'European' of North American cities, having joyously preserved and honoured the soul of its founding French and British culture. It's the largest French-speaking city in the world after Parisand Montréal is a city which exists in a balance between different worlds. It's firmly planted in North America, yet it gazes towards Europe and it is claimed by two differing entities in the form of French-speaking Québec and North American Canada. As a city, Montréal is difficult to define. At street level, its Gallic roots are the stronger of the two cultures. Although almost everyone is bilingual, French is the language of choice for the majority of the population and the city's impressive architecture is a clear reminder why this is the case. With busy sidewalk cafés, cobblestone streets, wrought-iron balconies and designer fashion boutiques, it could be an enclave of Paris.

A wander into historic Old Montréal is a throwback to the 17th century. It's a maze of narrow cobblestone streets winding past architectural masterpieces representing every era of the city's development, dating back to its foundation in 1642. The neo-gothic Notre Dame Basilica, opened in 1829, is perhaps the most impressive of all the sights in Old Montréal and a light show is held every evening showcasing the amazing exterior and interior. The city's backdrop is Mont Royale, a sprawling park with a split personality. During the hot summer months, it's a favourite place for joggers, walkers and rollerbladers, while in winter, when the snow hits, it transforms into a haven for cross country skiers. Whatever the weather, the locals celebrate and embrace life with a passion, and the café culture has strengthened the city's reputation for innovative and inspiring dining options. Overall, Montréal is a big city which has managed to hang on to its human touch, as well as its unique personality. Elusive and mysterious, visitors also quickly discover it's a very genuine city, even if they are only immersed in its culture for a few days.

SWEET SUCCESS

If you have ever poured maple syrup on your pancakes and wondered where this sweet, golden liquid comes from, you may be surprised to know that it actually comes from the sap of a maple tree. Compared to the maple syrup you may have in your pantry, maple sap is thin, colourless, and barely sweet. But the sugar in the sap is a mystery. It appears that each autumn, the tree produces sugar in the form of starch to act as an anti-freeze to protect its roots from the oncoming winter. As the snow melts, water penetrates the tree's roots and begins the circulation of a 'sugar water' through the tree ready for the growing season. With the spring thaw, enzymes change the starch in the water into sugar, which mixes with the water giving the sap its slightly sweet taste.

In the early days, processing maple syrup was a gruelling job, which involved boiling 150 litres (40 gallons) of sap over an open fire until it reduced to just under four litres (one gallon) of syrup. Today, it's no less of a serious business, although modern technology has made it less time consuming and labour intensive. A maple tree lasts for about 30 years but the harvest season may last only four to six weeks, with only 10 per cent of the sap collected each year. Each tree has to grow to a diameter of at least 30cm or 12in before it's tapped, but as the tree continues to grow, more taps can be added to a maximum of four.

Tapping doesn't do any permanent damage to the tree, and each tap yields an average of just under 38 litres or around 10 gallons of sap per season. But it still takes a lot of sap to reach the end result—around 113–190 litres (30–50 gallons) of sap makes a mere four litres (one gallon) of syrup.

Maple syrup can be boiled further to produce maple cream, maple sugar and maple candy, and they have multiple culinary uses. Aside from smothering pancakes and French toast, maple syrup can be used to sweeten apple sauce, milkshakes, coffee, hot toddies and fresh fruit, and can be mixed with butter to make a glaze for sweet potatoes or carrots. Maple cream can be spread on bread or toast and can be used as a filler for pastries and cake, and maple sugar can be used as an alternative to regular sugar in tea, coffee, on cereal and in cakes.

THE ST. LAWRENCE RIVER & SAGUENAY RIVER

Cruising the waters of Canada and New England in autumn is more than just a way of experiencing the change of colours in the foliage—it's also a passage back in time and one of the most pleasant ways of enjoying the natural beauty of this rugged part of the world. It's a cruise of two halves, the first half of which involves an exploration of one of the great Canadian rivers, the St. Lawrence River. This majestic waterway flows from the heart of the continent into the ocean, connecting the Great Lakes in central Canada with the Atlantic Ocean via the Gulf of St. Lawrence. It was named by navigator Jacques Cartier during his second trip to Canada in 1535, who arrived in the Gulf on the feast day of St. Lawrence.

From Montréal, the next destination along the river on most cruise itineraries is Québec City, and from down river the sight of this ancient city is nothing short of magical. It resembles a scene from a fairy tale; old stone houses wedged between cosy cafés and bistros, Gothic spires spiking the skyline and original centuries-old horse-drawn carriages clip-clopping down cobblestone streets. For first-time visitors, it's easy to feel transported back in time. Québec City is a small jewel with three facets: the colonial settlement on the riverbanks, the walled city atop the cliff that towers above, and the modern metropolis that has spread far outside the walls. Towering regally over the city is one of the world's most recognisable landmarks and hotels, le Château Frontenac, which revels in its 19th century grandeur and commands sweeping views of the St Lawrence River. Like neighbouring Montréal, the people of Québec City embrace their French history with a passion and celebrate living in this great city with an infectious exuberance. A compact city, it's a walker's dream. There's a photo opportunity on almost every corner, the aroma of baguettes and roasting coffee abounds and there are sweeping views of the hinterland from atop the walled city.

While navigating the St. Lawrence River, some ships take the time for a minor detour along the Saguenay River. It's a stunning fjord which slices northwest from the upper reaches of the St. Lawrence River through the heart of Québec. Bordered by steep cliffs and impenetrable forest, it has an abundance of pristine coves, tumbling waterfalls, and a significant landmark, the eight-metre-tall statue of Notre Dame de Saguenay, presiding over Trinity Bay from atop a cliff. The river was an important trade route into the interior of the Québec for the First Nations peoples of the area, and during the French colonisation of the Americas it was a major route for the fur trade. Today it is still an important artery for the state, as well as a popular site for breeding Beluga whales.

The St. Lawrence River drains into the Gulf of St. Lawrence and into the Atlantic Ocean, and from there the next major port of call is Halifax in Nova Scotia. Perched on the edge of one of the largest natural harbours in the world, Halifax has undergone a major transformation in recent years from a port town frequented by sea dogs to a world class tourist destination which has embraced its maritime past. Halifax has been a significant port since 1749 and a major strategic military hub, and it remains the modern heart of Atlantic Canada. Its numerous historic and cultural attractions are all within walking distance, from the imposing and perfectly preserved Citadel, an odd shaped fort which stands sentinel over the city and surrounds, to the Maritime Museum of the Atlantic, Maritime Command Museum, and the breathtaking harbour itself. A popular 'Kodak' moment is Peggy's Cove, a 45-minute drive from Halifax. It's a picturesque, if touristy, fishing village which is famous for a whitewashed lighthouse that doubles up as a post office. The journey through pristine countryside is impressive with mirror-like lakes, painted cottages, and a sweeping landscape with enough colours to make you feel like you're in an Edward Hopper watercolour.

LOBSTER WARS

Fans of the cult television program, *Lobster Wars*, have nothing but admiration for the incredible battles which modern lobstermen have to endure in order to catch their prize. In the depths of winter, fleets of lobster boats head out from North America's eastern seaboard into the North Atlantic, to a remote area where lobsters flock in huge numbers each year. From raging seas to freezing temperatures and everything in between, the crews of these boats literally risk life and limb to trap these prized pink crustaceans, so they can top the menu of pricey dishes offered up at expensive restaurants across the globe. Watching their riveting battles with nature, it's hard to imagine that lobster was once considered a poor man's food and it was even used as fertiliser and fish bait!

During the arrival of the first European settlers in North America, lobsters were abundant. Since they were were so plentiful in supply, they often provided a hearty meal for poor families who lived along the eastern coastline, as well as being harvested to feed prisoners and indentured servants who exchanged their passage to America for seven years of service to their sponsor. As a result, they were considered 'poverty food', and regarded with absolute disdain by the more affluent. In time, however, even the poor lost their appetite for lobster. In fact, in Massachusetts, some servants rebelled and had it written into their contracts that they would not be forced to eat lobster more than three times a week!

As the years passed, however, lobster's reputation for being a cheap eat declined, and by the 1840s, commercial fisheries in Maine, the largest lobster-producing state in the US, were in full swing to meet demand for the crustaceans. Over the years, this demand continued to increase, and the public's insatiable appetite for lobster eventually took its toll on lobster populations. Thanks to strict conservation measures, however, numbers of the Maine lobster are on the rise again, and the market is also being supplied by many varieties of lobster from countries including Mexico, Australia, South Africa and South America.

New England & New York

This region of the United States is located in the northeastern corner of the country and encompasses the states of Maine, New Hampshire, Vermont, Massachusetts, Rhode Island and Connecticut. It's one of the earliest English settlements in the New World, and pilgrims fleeing religious persecution in Europe first settled in these parts in the early 1600s in the colony of Plymouth. In the 19th century, the region played a major role in the movement to abolish slavery, and it was the first region of the United States to be transformed by the North American Industrial Revolution. From here to New York City, various destinations feature on cruise itineraries, offering passengers an opportunity to explore some of the country's most historic towns and cities. Bar Harbor is one, a quaint fishing village famous for lobster and the dramatic outdoor playground of Acadia National Park.

But one of the most popular destinations on the cruise route is Boston, a cosmopolitan city which combines modern sophistication with the old world charm of early Americana. Few cities juxtapose the old and the new like Boston does, with modern skyscrapers piercing the sky amid street after brick-sidewalked street of 18th and 19th century townhouses and churches. In Boston, sometimes it seems that everything has a historical marker attached to it, and the colonial granddaddy of them all is the Freedom Trail which starts on the Boston Common at Massachusetts State House. The trail links 16 historic sites including the Old State House, the Paul Revere House, old Burial Grounds, the site of the Boston Massacre and the Old North Church, and it's a walking tour that tells the story of Boston in the Revolutionary period.

Further south, Newport, Rhode Island, has arguably preserved Colonial industry and gilded-age splendour like no other place in the United States. In the modern era, however, it is the home of the America's Cup, as well as a playground for the fabulously wealthy. The cliffside walk offers great views of the fantastic yachts in harbour, and back from the water is where you'll find some of North America's most opulent and historic mansions. And finally, there's the city of New York, the enigmatic metropolis which marks the beginning, or the end, of most fall cruises. The largest city in the United States, founded by the Dutch in 1625 as a commercial trading post, it is located on one of the world's finest natural harbours. And for anyone who has been lucky to do it, sailing into New York's harbour, past Lady Liberty and beneath the shadows of the Manhattan skyline, is a sight to behold.

ABOVE: Seven Seas Mariner at Tracey Arm, Alaska

VIVACIOUS VANCOUVER

Cruising in Alaska often ends, or begins, in either Alaska's capital, Juneau, or Canada's cosmopolitan harbour city, Vancouver. Canada's biggest west coast city, Vancouver is situated just over the US border, and it's been widely described as the most scenic city in North America. Set on a magnificent harbour ringed by a wall of towering mountains, the city's densely packed skyscrapers compete for the blue sky, adding a touch of the modern to an already dramatic landscape. The smell of salt air mingles with the uplifting aroma of the surrounding forests, and Vancouver's natural beauty really gives it its northwest Pacific frontier feel. But down at street level there's a level of sophistication, without the pretentiousness of many other international cities. For anyone about to embark on an Alaska cruise, a stopover in Vancouver really sets the stage for the adventure to come.

There's plenty to see and do. For a start, you can explore the city's wide open space, Stanley Park, which is bigger than New York's Central Park. And another popular pastime is taking one of the city's mini-ferries, called aquabuses, to Granville Island which is home to Vancouver's biggest market. Back in the centre of town, Yaletown has undergone a major facelift in recent years and is now a trendy neighbourhood with renovated warehouses and hip bars. In contrast, historic Gastown marks the start of modern-day Vancouver and was the site of the founding of the city in 1870. It's also home to the famous Steam Clock, one of the most photographed landmarks in the city. For a panoramic view of the city and its environs, however, the place to head for is Grouse Mountain, a ski resort which operates year-round. The eight-minute tram ride to the peak is invigorating in itself, and at the top there are hiking trails and an endangered wildlife sanctuary, as well as that view.

Alaska

It's nearly 10pm and outside the clouds hovering over the mountain light the sky with a silver hue. In the distance a glacier reflects the light like a beacon, and the air is cool and still. Below the ship's hull the water is calm, and in the dim light it's possible to catch a glimpse of a snow-capped peak. Welcome to Alaska, a vast Pacific Northwest wilderness twice the size of Texas, that possesses over 76,000km (47,000 miles) of rugged shoreline and four million acres of national parklands. It's a vast land of dramatic landscapes and is teeming with wildlife. Travelling north from the vibrant Canadian city of Vancouver, hundreds of cruise ships ply the waters of Alaska's famed Inside Passage during the short northern hemisphere summer. Here, ships have to negotiate their way around hundreds of tiny islands and at times you are so close to the land either side of the waterway, that you feel you could almost reach out and touch the firs and pine trees.

Shaped by the incredible force of massive glaciers millions of years ago, Alaska's Inside Passage provides travellers with a unique cruising experience. It's a dramatic landscape draped with lush scenery, towering peaks, deep fjords, remote islands and abundant wildlife. It may be a victim of its success, with more and more ships and tourists visiting each year, but it remains a memorable destination for its sheer scale and diversity. The ultimate lure of an Alaskan cruise is nature itself, with a pair of binoculars an essential accessory. During the summer months it's possible to spot all manner of marine life including humpback whales, sea lions, and porpoises. In the air, American bald eagles can be frequently spotted gliding out of the clouds and on the shoreline caribou stand grazing seemingly metres from the deck of the ship.

BELOW: Cruising Alaska's Inside Passage (Photo: Barry Hopkins)

COLD AS ICE

A cruise to Alaska will undoubtedly involve an up-close-and-personal encounter with a glacier, either from the deck of the ship, or a fly-by in a small plane or helicopter. A glacier is made up of fallen snow that, over many years, compresses into a large, thickened mass of ice. Some glaciers are as small as football fields, while others can grow to be over a hundred kilometers long. What makes glaciers unique, however, is their ability to move. This is because of their sheer mass, and gravity, and they flow like very slow rivers. Some, called tide water glaciers, flow into the ocean. Alaska has more active glaciers than the rest of the world combined, almost 100,000, and Southeast Alaska has 60 major glaciers alone. The glaciers of Prince William Sound and Southeast Alaska's Inside Passage are the most accessible from cruise ships, and if you're really lucky, you may see a glacier calve—that's when a large chunk of ice breaks off and falls into the ocean. But these chunks of ice are different from normal ice; they weigh thousands of kilos, they can be a large as a small house and they appear to be blue rather than white. If you are really lucky, however, Glacier Bay may feature on your itinerary. Here, 16 spectacular glaciers flow from surrounding mountains into the icy waters of Glacier Bay National Park and Preserve.

BELOW: Hubbard Glacier, Alaska, at sunset

NEXT PAGE
Alaska's Hubbard Glacier (Photo: Barry Hopkins)

THE NORTHERN REGION

Alaska's state capital, Juneau, is the dominant destination in the northern half of the Inside Passage. A small, picturesque city perched on the Gastineau Channel, it's a dramatic spot where towering mountain peaks cascade down to the sea. In fact, this mountain range makes the city inaccessible by car, and Juneau is the only US state capital which is literally cut off from the world by road, and the only way in, or out, is by ship or plane. As a popular destination to start, or finish, an Alaska cruise, during the summer months it often appears full to bursting point. But the city and surrounds have many alluring sights and activities to offer visitors. The tramway up Mt. Roberts provides great views across the city, the mountain tops and the Inside Passage.

Juneau is in the middle of the northernmost rainforest in the world, and water forms the critical link that ties everything together. Visitors can get out on the water to fish for salmon or halibut, or go rafting in the Mendenhall River. And from the air, flightseeing offers a bird's-eye view of Juneau's dramatic scenery, including the unique drama of flying over the Juneau Icefield. But Juneau's most popular attraction is undoubtedly the magnificent Mendenhall Glacier. Located just 21km (13 miles) from the downtown area, many cruise ships visit this natural wonder en-route to or from Juneau and 'park' right beside it, giving passengers an up-close-and-personal encounter with the famous blue ice. Everything about this glacier is impressive; it's face stands over 30 metres (100 feet), it's almost 2.5km (1.5 miles) wide, and it flows out of the Mendenhall Valley for 9.5km (6 miles). And yet Mendenhall Glacier is just a tiny part of the Juneau Icefield, an expanse of glaciers which have linked together behind the mountain range next to Juneau.

North of Juneau, the town of Yakutat is the jumping off point for a visit to one of Alaska's famous tidewater glaciers, the Hubbard Glacier. From its source, this impressive glacier stretches 122km (76 miles) to the sea at Yakutat Bay and Disenchantment Bay. It is the longest tidewater glacier in Alaska, with an open calving face over 10km (6 miles) wide. Also north of Juneau is Skagway, a small, town with a history centred around the Klondike Gold Rush. In 1898, 20,000 prospectors passed through the town in search of Klondike gold, and the era's history has been carefully preserved though the town's colourful storefronts and the famous Chilkoot and White Pass Trails, the routes which the thousands of prospectors took from Yukon. In Sitka, which nestles on the mountainous Baranof Island, history of a different kind has been preserved. Dubbed the Russian capital of Alaska from 1808 to 1867, when ownership was transferred back to the United States, it is a multicultural city with an impressive backdrop in the towering, snow-capped Mont Edgecumbe.

CHEFS AT SEA, MICHEL RICHARD

Michel Richard is the celebrated chef and founder of the esteemed Michel Richard Citronelle in Washington, D.C. This highly acclaimed chef has many accolades to his name including membership of the prestigious Relais & Chateau from 2003 to 2007. Citronelle has been described as 'one of the world's most exciting restaurants' by *Condé Nast Traveler* magazine, and one of the 10 American 'restaurants that count' by the *New York Times*. Richard's unique culinary genius combines class French techniques with New World Food. It's a gastronomic fusion of art, innovation, freshness and lightness. In July last year, he was a guest chef on Regent Seven Seas Cruises, sailing for the first time on the Seven Seas Mariner in Alaska. The cruise was a seven-day voyage from Seward to Vancouver with a spotlight on food and wine. In addition to sharing his love of food with guests through cooking demonstrations, Richard also created a special tasting menu which featured Tomato Tartare With Gruyere Chips (see recipe).

'I heard my calling when I first caught a glimpse of a restaurant kitchen at the age of eight. The white hats, aprons, and all of the food, I fell in love. People ask me about the challenges of cooking on a cruise ship, and I guess there is always a challenge when you work with staff you don't know. Usually, it will take cooking a new dish four or five times to train employees. On a cruise ship, you have to train all the employees in two days. It's like the first day when you open a new restaurant, and then it's all over, and if you succeed then it's great. Another challenge is that you can't always get fresh ingredients every day. But there are wonderful chefs on board, who do everything they can to please the guest chef and the guests. They are dedicated and passionate people who try their best, and they are proud to work with a guest chef.'

SOUTHERN REGION

The southern half of the Inside Passage stretches from Prince of Wales Island in the south, to Kake in the north. Prince of Wales Island is the third largest island in the United States, and it offers visitors a true taste of the wilderness, with mountains dominating the landscape and a network of streams flowing in all directions. This island is a place where spotting wildlife is as guaranteed as it can ever be, with bears, deer, eagles, herons, whales and sea lions all calling this section of the Inside Passage home. Travelling north from Prince of Wales Island, there are a number of fascinating destinations to visit and sights to see. Ketchikan is the southernmost point for most ships, a town which sprawls along the coast of Revillagigedo Island for several kilometres and has the distinctively-shaped Deer Mountain to its south. A bustling community with a backdrop of impressive forested hills and surrounded by water, it hums energetically with the sounds of fishing boats, seaplanes and ferries. The heart of the town is centred on a single road, Tongass Avenue, which runs along the shores of Tongass Narrows, and sometimes over it, on a road supported by pillars. Of the many sights to see, the Totem Heritage Center is the place where dozens of original Tlingit totem poles have been have salvaged and restored to their original condition.

Further north, Wrangell is a town with a past which was shaped by four groups of people: the Russians, the English, the Americans and the Tlingit. One of the oldest non-Native settlements in Alaska, it thrived as a supply centre for fur traders and then gold miners. One of Wrangell's most interesting attractions is Chief Snakes Island, which is located in the town's inner Boat Harbor and accessed by a bridge. It has a collection of impressive totem poles and is home of the Shakes Community House, an excellent example of a high-caste tribal house complete with tools, blankets and other cultural artifacts. In Petersburg, which sits on the northwest tip of Mitkof Island, the locals embrace their Norwegian heritage with decorative Norwegian painting on the houses and storefronts, as well as a four-day Little Norway festival each May. This is widely regarded as one of Alaska's hidden jewels, a busy town which doubles as a fishing port, and which is marked by the brightly painted buildings and the snow-capped peaks shimmering on the horizon. Just 40km (25 miles) away is the LeConte Glacier, the southernmost active tidewater glacier in North America, and yet another of the Inside Passage's most dramatic sights.

BELOW: Seven Seas Mariner stops to watch orcas in Alaska's Inside Passage

Cocktails

Manhattan

2 parts Jim Beam Bourbon
1 part sweet vermouth
A dash of Angostura Bitters
A maraschino cherry to garnish

Stir ingredients gently in a mixing glass with ice, strain into a large martini glass, drop cherry into the bottom and serve.

Cosmopolitan

4 parts vodka
1 part Cointreau
1 part fresh lime juice
1 part cranberry juice

Mix all ingredients in a cocktail shaker with ice, strain, and serve in a large martini glass.

RIGHT: Manhattan

Recipes

Classic Chicken Caesar Salad

2 chicken breasts, skin off
½ to ¾ cup croutons
½ cup mayonnaise
1 to 2 garlic cloves, finely chopped
1 anchovy fillet mashed
4 anchovy fillets cut in half
Pinch of coarse sea salt
2 tbsp freshly squeezed lemon juice
A dash of Worcestershire Sauce
3 tbsp extra-virgin olive oil
¼ cup freshly grated Parmesan cheese
1 head Romaine lettuce
Coarsely ground black pepper

Start by pan-frying the chicken breasts. When cooked, cut into pieces and set aside to cool. Then separate the Romaine leaves (discarding the coarse outer leaves). Wash, drain, and dry them, then cut them into small pieces before refrigerating.

Next, make the dressing. In a bowl, mix together the garlic, anchovy, and salt, and whisk until blended, then add the lemon juice and Worcestershire sauce. Add mayonnaise and continue whisking until the mixture is thick. Drizzle in the olive oil in small amounts at a time, whisking in between, and finally add and whisk in half of the Parmesan cheese.

In a large wooden salad bowl, add a third of the dressing and toss with the croutons until well coated. Add the leaves, chicken pieces, anchovy fillets, and the remaining dressing, and toss well. Serve onto chilled plates, or in bowls, sprinkling each serving with the remaining Parmesan cheese, and some pepper.

Serves 2 to 4

Chocolate Fudge Sheba with Raspberry Sauce

570g (1¼lb) bittersweet or semisweet chocolate, coarsely chopped
6 egg yolks
1 cup unsalted butter at room temperature
9 egg whites, at room temperature
1½ cups sugar

Raspberry sauce
½ cup of water
1 punnet of fresh raspberries
Cornstarch if required

Butter a large loaf pan around 22 x 12 cm (9 x 5 in) in size. Place ¾ of the chocolate in a bowl, and place into a large pan of simmering water to melt gently. Stir until smooth. Transfer the chocolate to another bowl and allow to cool. Place the egg yolks in a bowl, place the bowl into the large pan of simmering water, and whisk the egg yolks until thick and pale. Remove the bowl from the pan, and whisk until completely cool.

Using an electric mixer, beat the butter in a large bowl until fluffy. Then, using a spatula, fold in the melted chocolate, followed by the egg yolks. Using the electric mixer (with clean beaters), beat the egg whites until soft peaks begin to form. Add the sugar a little at a time, and beat until whites become stiff and shiny and form a meringue. Fold the meringue into chocolate mixture, pour the mixture into the loaf pan, and top with the remaining chopped chocolate. Then cover and refrigerate until set.

To make the raspberry sauce, crush the raspberries with water in a saucepan, add the sugar and bring to the boil stirring constantly. If the mixture doesn't thicken enough, add a little cornstarch until the desired consistency is reached. Reduce heat and simmer for 2 minutes, then push through a strainer. Before serving, remove the Sheba from the fridge and allow to soften slightly. To serve, cut into thin slices and serve with a drizzle of the raspberry sauce and a fresh raspberry.

Serves 12 to 16

Fillet Steak with Prawns

4 fillet steaks
4 large prawns, peeled with tails on
8 large cherry or plum tomatoes
2 cups of shiitake mushrooms
a bunch of green asparagus
1 tbsp of extra-virgin olive oil
4 medium mashing potatoes
½ tsp salt
2 tbsp thick cream
1 tbsp butter
Salt and pepper
4 sprigs of rosemary
4 large coarse-cut pain potato chips

Red wine sauce
½ glass red wine
¼ cup beef stock
⅓ cup hot water
2 tbsp butter

Start by cooking the potatoes in water with ½ teaspoon of salt. When cooked, drain off the water, place in a bowl, and mash with a potato masher. Melt the butter in a saucepan, add the cream and mix. Fold the cream and butter into the potato using a large, strong spoon until smooth and creamy.

Then, in a saucepan, boil some water and add the whole tomatoes. Remove as soon as the skin starts to peel off and set aside. Remove the heads of the asparagus, add to a frying pan with the mushrooms, and gently stir fry using a little olive oil. Set aside when cooked. In the same pan, gently fry the steak to the desired temperature. Then add the prawns and cook for about a minute.

In a saucepan, mix the wine, beef stock, and water, and bring to the boil. Simmer for two minutes, before adding the butter, and mix until thick and glossy. Then brown the chips briefly under a grill.

To serve, place each steak on a plate, place a prawn on top of the steak, and then a scoop of potato on top of each prawn. Garnish with a sprig of rosemary and a potato chip. Then drizzle a little of the red wine sauce around each steak, and surround with two of the tomatoes and an even number of the mushrooms and asparagus heads.

Serves four

New England Clam Chowder

4 slices of lean bacon, fat removed
½ cup of whole milk
400g (14 oz) canned clams, minced
2 medium potatoes
1 small onion
2 tbsp butter
2 tbsp flour
1 cup single cream
Salt and pepper to taste
Crackers

First, cut the potatoes into quarters and boil until cooked. Once cooked, cut into small cubes and set aside. Then cook the bacon in olive oil until crisp, chop into small pieces and set aside. Dice the onion, cook in the same pan until soft and set aside. Take a saucepan and heat the milk to a gentle boil.

Add the butter and stir until blended, then add the cream and finally the flour to thicken.

Add the clams and continue to simmer over a low heat for a few minutes.

Finally, add the potatoes, the onion and salt and pepper to taste.

To serve, divide between six bowls and serve with the crackers of your choice.

Serves six

Tomato Tartar with Gruyere Chips

(Supplied by Chef Michel Richard)

12 large Roma tomatoes
3 tbsp finely minced shallots
1 small beet cooked and diced
1 garlic clove
1 tsp Dijon mustard
1 tsp soy sauce
½ tsp granulated sugar
1 tsp drained capers, chopped
1 tsp minced chives
1 tsp extra virgin olive oil
Fine sea salt and freshly ground
Black pepper to taste
Tabasco sauce to taste
8 Gruyere chips

Shallot dressing
½ cup mayonnaise
½ tsp Dijon mustard
¼ cup finely minced shallots
1 tbsp red wine vinegar
1 tbsp water
4 drops Tabasco sauce
¼ cup minced chives
¼ cup chopped basil
Fine sea salt and freshly ground
black pepper to taste.

Preheat the oven to 120°C (250°F). Line a baking sheet with a silicone mat or parchment. First, cook the beet in water for half an hour, strain, reduce juice to half, and keep the juice aside. Then, cut out and discard the cores from the tomatoes, cut each one lengthwise in half and place cut side up on the baking sheet. Slow-roast for 3 hours to partially dry the tomatoes.

Next, bring a small pan of water to the boil, add the shallots and blanch quickly. Drain in a fine-mesh sieve, run cold water over to cool them down, and dry on a paper towel. Take the tomatoes out of the oven, remove the skins and scoop out the seedy centers, leaving tomato 'shells'. Chop the tomato flesh, place in the centre of a piece of cheesecloth, hold over a bowl, and wring out to remove the excess liquid. Place the tomatoes in a medium bowl. Add the shallots to the tomatoes, and one tablespoon of the beet juice to 'colour' the tomato to look like beef. Mince the garlic directly into the bowl, add the remaining ingredients, and refrigerate the tartare until it is cold.

To make the Gruyere chips, preheat the oven to 120°C (250°F), and line a baking sheet with a silicone mat. Cut 8 very thick slices of Gruyere, arrange on the sheet, leaving about 5 cms (2in) between them, and bake for about 15 minutes until the cheese has melted and browned to a golden brown. Remove from the oven and let the chips firm up. When they are easy to remove, lift them with a spatula and place on paper towels to cool.

Place all of the ingredients for the shallot dressing in a blender, and blend until smooth. To serve, place a 7 cm (3in) ring mold in the center of a serving plate and fill loosely with one-quarter of the tartare. Remove the mold and repeat on three more plates. Spoon the shallot dressing around each tartare, sprinkle with chives, and garnish with 2 Gruyere chips.

Serves four

02:

Eastern Mediterranean

*I*t's the home of some of the great ancient civilisations where history and mythology combine. The Eastern Mediterranean is a heady mix of fantastic architecture and monuments, sun-drenched beaches and the deep blue of the sea which itself was the scene of bloody battles of a massive scale between warring empires. It's a region which was, and still is, a crucial maritime trade route for the great civilisations. Greek, Roman, Egyptian, Mesopotamian, Phoenician and Moorish traders, among many, shaped the Eastern Mediterranean into its modern day guise. These empires have risen and fallen, and borders have been moved and removed, but the societies built around the sea remain congruous in their maritime culture. The Latin word *mediterraneus* means 'middle of the Earth' and even today this reverence for, and dependance on the waterway remains. This is where you can walk the cobblestone streets of ancient cities, swim in a deserted bay, experience fantastic museums and cathedrals and stand before magnificent antiquities with the added bonus of a new cultural experience almost every day.

Turkey

ISTANBUL

As the sun drops and casts a warm orange hue across the city, the now-familiar 'Call to Prayer' reverberates across the Bosphorus River from one of the many mosques that dominate the skyline. Traditional ferryboats cruise past carrying a mix of office workers on their way home and suburbanites heading for an evening out, and on the outside decks many of the locals are sipping tea and taking in the magnificent view.

In the distance, the Topkapi Palace, the Basilica of Saint Sophia and the Blue Mosque change colour as they're lit up for the evening, as if to confirm these are the city's crown jewels. After just a day in Istanbul, sensory overload has already kicked in and it's no wonder this place is routinely called one of the great cities of Europe...and Asia. Straddling the imposing Bosphorus River which serves as a geographic border, Istanbul literally has a foot in each continent and is at the crossroads of the Western and Islamic worlds.

For thousands of years it's been a maritime city of great historical and strategic importance which began when the early Greeks founded the city as Byzantium in 658 BC. Since then the Persians, Alexander the Great, the Roman Empire and modern Turkish conquerors were some of the world's great empires which claimed Istanbul as their own. Sailing into, or out of, Istanbul is an experience which goes some way towards gaining a sense of its rich history, and most cruises start and/or finish in this city because of the grand scale of its presence.

Many volumes have been written about Istanbul's fascinating and historic past. Over 26 centuries, emperors, kings and sultans have all passed through Istanbul and left their mark on this vast, bustling metropolis, packed with remnants of past imperial might. The English writer Sir Sacheverell Sitwell summed up the grandeur of Istanbul in *Arabesque and Honeycomb* in 1957: 'Our ship makes a sweep towards it and in that moment we see before and in front of us the opening of the Golden Horn, and one after another all the Imperial Mosques of Istanbul standing against and upon the skyline. It is the most sensational revelation: one after another of these great domes as in a panorama, they stand there like huge kettledrums with something menacing and martial in their air, and in that moment it is more of a capital than any other city, more than London, or than Rome, or Paris.'

KUSADASI & EPHESUS

Istanbul aside, one of Turkey's most popular tourist destinations is the ancient city of Ephesus, which is the best preserved Aegean antiquity, and its intact state makes it one of the most important archaeological sites in the world. Wandering the smooth marble streets gives a very real sense of what life was like in ancient Greece or Rome.

Kusadasi is the port that provides access to Ephesus, which is about 12km away, and the former has been transformed from a sleepy fishing town into a busy tourist hub thanks to the increasing number of cruise ships visiting the region. While Kusadasi is not everyone's cup of tea because of the persistent and insistent hawkers, including rug sellers, just a short distance away is the best preserved classical city of the Eastern Mediterranean.

Ephesus was founded around 3000BC, and the empires of Greece, Persia, Rome, Byzantium and the Ottoman Turks at various times reigned over the city. At its peak in the second century AD it was the second largest city in the Roman Empire, behind Rome. At that time it was home to more than 250,000 people and was one of the most important ports in Europe with goods passing through from Asia to Greece and Italy. Perhaps the city's greatest claim to fame is its temple to the goddess Artemis, which is one of the Seven Wonders of the Ancient World. It was almost four times the size of the Parthenon in Athens and sadly today only a few original columns remain.

Despite that, there is still enough ancient grandeur in Ephesus, including the Great Theatre which is built into the side of a hill and seated 25,000 people at one stage. It sits near Harbor Way and it's hard to believe that Ephesus once had a harbour, as it's now about 8km (5 miles) from the ocean, which silted up over time and perhaps led to the city's ultimate demise. It can take anything from a few hours to a full day to explore Ephesus and it's worth paying for an English-speaking guide or buying a guide book, and the best place to start is at the Magnesian Gate which is at the top of a hill. It means the exploration of the city is mostly a downhill walk which is an absolute godsend especially if the weather is hot, as it usually is.

Walking along Curettes Way, lined with the remains of a colonnade that shaded pedestrians, and ahead is another of the highlights of Ephesus, the Library of Celsus.

ABOVE: Library of Celsus, Ephesus, Turkey

The grand marble road leads down to one of the largest libraries of the ancient world which contained between 12,000 and 15,000 scrolls. The library was built between 110AD and 135AD in memory of Roman Senator Celsus Polemeanus, who was Proconsul of the Province of Asia. The facade of the Library has been restored to its original condition and its importance is that it's one of the few remaining ancient Roman libraries which mostly followed the same classical architecture. At the entrance to the Library is a 21 metre wide (23 yards) courtyard paved in marble, and nine wide marble steps lead up to the main entrance. The tomb of Celsus remains inside and his life is celebrated in Greek and Latin on the bases of statues on each side of the library staircase.

Other ruins include the Odeon, a small theatre built around 150AD which hosted smaller plays and concerts for up to two thousand people. It originally had a closed roof, and the upper part of the theatre was decorated with red granite pillars. The Temple of Hadrian on Curettes Way was also built in the second century and is one of the more beautiful ruins and inside the temple is a relief of Medusa, and a frieze depicting gods and other mythological figures connected with the city. The Temple of Domitian is on a square where shops and stores once flourished and this was one of the biggest temples in Ephesus. The State Agora or Town Hall occupies a massive piece of land which included a courtyard which led into the main building and contained different rooms and halls where city officials met.

This is all just 15 per cent of the city and excavations are continuing, with experts predicting that the project which began at the end of the 19th century will continue for 'hundreds of years more'.

THE MODERN-DAY RIDDLE OF THE SPHINX

One of the highlights of many Eastern Mediterranean cruises is a stop at the port of Alexandria in Egypt, affording passengers the opportunity of a day-trip to see the Pyramids of Giza, including the only remaining of the Seven Ancient Wonders of the World, the Great Pyramid. As your bus sweeps down into the dusty valley, with the bustling city of Cairo as a backdrop, seeing the three giant pyramids for the first time draws inevitable gasps. But a personal favourite photo opportunity of ours is the view back at the pyramids from down the valley at the site of the Great Sphinx. The word sphinx, which means 'strangler' was first given by the Greeks to an exotic creature which had the head of a woman, the body of a lion, and the wings of a bird. In Egypt, however, there are numerous sphinxes, usually with the head of a king adorned with a headdress, and the body of a lion.

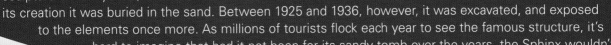

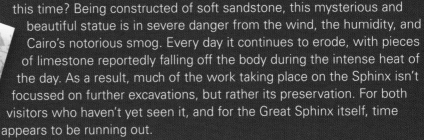

The Sphinx is said to be the most immense stone sculpture made by man, and over the centuries since its creation it was buried in the sand. Between 1925 and 1936, however, it was excavated, and exposed to the elements once more. As millions of tourists flock each year to see the famous structure, it's hard to imagine that had it not been for its sandy tomb over the years, the Sphinx wouldn't be here today. But the burning question for many experts is: how long will it last this time? Being constructed of soft sandstone, this mysterious and beautiful statue is in severe danger from the wind, the humidity, and Cairo's notorious smog. Every day it continues to erode, with pieces of limestone reportedly falling off the body during the intense heat of the day. As a result, much of the work taking place on the Sphinx isn't focussed on further excavations, but rather its preservation. For both visitors who haven't yet seen it, and for the Great Sphinx itself, time appears to be running out.

PREVIOUS PAGE
LEFT: The Great Sphinx and Pyramid of Khafre
RIGHT: Bedouin camel riders at Giza

RIGHT: The Crystal Symphony at anchor off the Island of Santorini, Greek Islands

The Greek Islands

With more than 6,000 islands and islets scattered haphazardly across the Aegean and Ionian Seas, the Greek Islands have become synonymous with great beaches, wonderful food, unique wines, friendly people, and a fascinating and rich history which is heavily influenced by its maritime surroundings. Around 230 of the islands are actually inhabited, and combined they provide the most diverse landscapes of any island group with thousands of kilometres of beaches with black sand, white sand and pebbles, sheltered by stunning bays and coves, volcanic mountains, lush forests, deserts, and of course the deep blue of the Mediterranean. The Greek Islands almost always feature on Eastern Mediterranean cruises and two of the most popular destinations are Santorini in the Cyclades and Rhodes in the Dodecanese group.

SANTORINI

Of all the Greek islands, Santorini stands out for its natural beauty which was created out of a cataclysmic event 3,500 years ago when a volcanic eruption wiped out all human life on the island and in the cities of nearby Crete. It's believed to have been largely responsible for the demise of the mighty Minoan civilisation. Three quarters of Santorini's land mass vanished, and the nearby islands of Palaia Kameni and Nea Kameni were pushed up higher and formed the dramatic caldera which is now filled with water.

Ancient writers, including Plato, claimed this eruption and others that followed brought an end to the utopian city of Atlantis and although this has been disproved, wandering the cobbled alleys and cliff top paths could convince the most unimaginative that the theory had some credibility. The island still undergoes eruptions periodically, the last in 1956, and the ancient Santorini residents accepted the fact that the island would need to fight the gods of earth and fire to win the battles against the volcanoes and earthquakes.

Most visitors to Santorini arrive by ferry, and the natural phenomenon is undoubtedly best seen from the ocean, and is also an unforgettable experience from a cruise ship or one of the tour boats that run day trips around the islands. From the ocean, the sheer scale of the towering volcanic cliffs is put well and truly in perspective, as is the realisation that you're actually floating above an active volcano and perched along the rim of the dramatic caldera are whitewashed homes, churches, cafés, restaurants and hotels with arguably the most stunning views in the world. On land, the main town of Fira can be over-run with tourists and backpackers in the peak season from June to August, but outside of this time it does become more genteel and relaxed, despite the abundance of tourist shops.

A 20–30 minute moped trip away to the north is the quieter and more refined town of Oia, which seems to have avoided the trappings of mass tourism with a different set of bylaws that limit the numbers of bars and late night music. The large neoclassical homes have been rebuilt, as have the traditional fishermen's homes built centuries ago, and this town of just over 1,000 seems to exist in a world of its own. Its sunsets are legendary with the main point looking directly west, and every day hundreds of tourists and locals sit quietly and wait for the highlight of the day in this part of the world. There's not actually that much to do in Oia, and apart from the Maritime Museum, a typical day revolves around where to have breakfast, lunch and a fish dinner and which rock to sit on to watch the sunset.

The beaches of Santorini are also an attraction in their own right and are generally typically Mediterranean with bright blue water and volcanic rocks. They range from the tourist resorts of Perissa and Kamari and the famous Red Beach, to the quieter Cape Columbo, Perivolos and Agios Georgios. North-east of Oia, Sigalas Winery provides a fun and interesting taste of Santorini wines which somehow thrive in this arid environment. Prices are cheap and can be sampled with a cheese platter. Despite being over-run with tourists in the peak season, the locals themselves remain cheerful and are proud of their stunning island home. They appear happy to pass on any insider knowledge of where to eat and where the quiet beaches are, but the island is so compact and welcoming you'll feel like one of the locals within a very short time.

RHODES

The island of Rhodes has a reputation as a sensual, sub-tropical paradise but it also possesses one of the best preserved medieval cities in Europe, and it's a combination of a hedonist's hangout and a history buff's fantasy come-to-life. Surrounded by medieval walls with seven magnificent gates, entering Rhodes Old Town is a step back into more than two thousand years of history, with fantastic and well preserved monuments, squares and houses, but that's not to say it's one big museum. Six thousand people live inside the walls and they give a real sense of life to a city which is a joy to discover.

True, there are restaurants, bars and cafés scattered throughout the Old Town, but even with a little imagination it's not hard to imagine that this is a place that has changed little for hundreds of years. The third largest Greek island, Rhodes is well known as a great place for sun worshippers looking for an idyllic beach retreat, but few people realise it's also home to the World Heritage listed medieval city, framed by its ancient harbour which was founded two and a half thousand years ago.

Archaeologists believe that one of the Seven Wonders of the Ancient World, the Colossus of Rhodes, stood sentinel over the harbour and the city until an earthquake destroyed it in 226BC. The Colossus was confirmation of the fact that Rhodes was an important economic centre in the ancient world thanks to its location where the Aegean Sea meets the Mediterranean.

Like most of the Mediterranean islands, Rhodes' history is essentially a long chronological list of conquerors and occupiers dating back to 408BC when the local islanders founded the city. Their independence came to an end in 164BC when Rhodes became a province of the Roman Empire, although its culture remained intact and it developed into one of the great centres of learning, science and the arts.

From the seventh century there were periodic attacks by Muslim invaders and in 1309, Rhodes was sold to the Order of the Knights Hospitaliers of Saint John of Jerusalem. Initially designed to nurse pilgrims and crusaders, the Order became a specialised fighting unit and the fortifications that now stand were built mostly during this period. In 1522 the Ottoman Turks finally conquered the city and built mosques and public baths, in 1912 Italian troops took over, in 1948 it became a part of Greece, and in 1988 it gained a UNESCO World Heritage listing which has resulted in a lot of excavation of old ruins and restoration of existing architecture.

Down at street level entering the Old Town through one of the Gates is like stepping into another world. Exploration of the city can be done in a day, although that can be a little overwhelming in a place that probably warrants three days at least. The first thing you notice when you arrive is the formidable city walls from the 15th century which were extended and fortified by the Knights over a period of 200 years. They're 12 metres (13 yards) thick with a moat that's 21 metres (23 yards) wide, and it runs to around 4km (2.5 miles) around the Old Town. The moats themselves no longer have water in them and instead they've been landscaped into beautiful gardens with walking paths.

RIGHT: Rhodes Old Town

NEXT PAGE
LEFT ABOVE: Palace of the Grand Master, Rhodes
LEFT BELOW: Rhodes Old Town leafy balcony
RIGHT: Main entrance to the Palace of the Grand Master, Rhodes

Inside the city and probably the most impressive building is the Palace of the Grand Master of the Knights of Rhodes which was built in the 14th century. Impressive on the outside, inside the enormous palace are relics from the medieval period as well as ancient sculptures and ornate first century floor mosaics.

Away from the palace, the walls contain an endless array of bastions, battlements, towers and gates, set among imposing buildings with beautiful decorations, paved courtyards, classic churches and imposing mosques, and museums.

Set just back from this unique setting are the residential areas of the Old Town, including the Jewish Quarter, and this is where beautiful rose window gardens catch the sunlight. Old men sip coffee and play backgammon in the middle of the street and the occasional moped is the only sound to break the serene atmosphere. It's a place that is most beautiful in the early evening when the harshness of the sun drops and casts a warm hue over the houses which date back to the Middle Ages.

Although the economy of the whole island is geared towards tourism, it is possible to experience an authentic slice of Greek cuisine and culture in some of these back streets. Many of the bars and restaurants around the major sights are geared towards foreign tourists, and their prices reflect this, but the local joints still exist and can be found just off the beaten path.

It's here that you'll find a good Turkish coffee, selections of mezes, real moussaka, local seafood and an atmosphere that is decidedly Mediterranean, and it's the perfect way to round off a visit to one of the truly unique cities of Europe.

GREEK WINE

Greece is famous for many things: great philosophers, the Acropolis, ouzo and the larger than life popular singer, Demis Roussos. One thing it isn't especially famous for is internationally respected wine, yet it may surprise many people to learn that Greece is actually one of the oldest wine-producing regions in the world. The origins of wine making there go back some 6,500 years, and the expansion of Greek civilisation and their worship of Dionysus, the great god of wine, spread rapidly throughout the Mediterranean during the period of 1600 BC to the year 0. As a result, wine has been an important and integral part of Greek culture for over 4,000 years. One of the things which makes Greek wines so unique is that there are more than 300 indigenous grape varieties grown in the country, both red and white, which produce a large number of highly distinctive flavours. One of the most well-known wine varieties is retsina, which became a national beverage during the 1960s, and is regarded by many as a defining part of the Greek wine culture. There are a number of wine growing regions in Greece, the primary ones being in the Aegean Islands including Crete, Rhodes and Santorini, Central Greece, Kefalonia in the Ionian Islands, Macedonia and Peloponnesus.

ATHENS

As the cradle of western democracy and culture, Athens' legacy makes it one of the most important cities in the world and fortunately much of the physical evidence of this remains as well and is being preserved for future generations. This is where government, law, architecture, philosophy, science, medicine, religion and the arts were formed, along with the more basic concept of civic life, and walking the streets of modern Athens reveals this is where the building blocks of western society were laid.

It's serviced by the ancient port of Piraeus, which at just 12km (7.5 miles) from the city centre appears to have seamlessly merged with the metropolis. These days Athens is one of the most popular destinations on cruise ship itineraries in the Mediterranean, not just for its superb ancient monuments and museums, but also for its bustling outdoor café and restaurant scene which thrives on a refreshing attitude that life is for living, and work is just a means to an end.

On the surface the city can resemble a chaotic mass of unplanned buildings, and heavy traffic in parts often causes smog, but in the heart of Athens major historical sites and dining and entertainment areas are linked by pedestrianised areas which provide an escape from the vehicular madness.

Standing sentinel over Athens, and dominating the cityscape from miles around, is the famous rocky crag known as the Acropolis. The 70m (230ft) high limestone fortress is the greatest symbol of the Classical Era with a multitude of monuments and artistic creations including the Parthenon, the greatest and most dramatic Doric Temple ever built. Completed in the 5th Century BC when the city was at its peak during the Golden Age of Perikles, the Parthenon was dedicated to the goddess of the city, Athena, and today it remains the unmistakeable symbol of Athens and is perhaps the most important monument in Europe. It's undergoing a major renovation which began in 1983 and will continue indefinitely, and despite the scaffolding, its splendour remains. As the poet Ralph Waldo Emerson wrote: 'Earth proudly wears the Parthenon as the best gem upon her zone.'

Within the Acropolis are at least half a dozen ancient masterpieces including the Erechtheion, a temple built in honour of both Athena and Poseidon, who according to mythology battled for patronage of Athens on that spot, the Temple of Athena Nike, the Propylaia or entrance to the Acropolis, the 17,000-seat Theatre of Dionysus and the Herodes Atticus Theatre.

At the foot of the Acropolis are the districts of Plaka and Monastiraki which are made up of small winding streets which are a delight to wander. Plaka is an historic area which has been gentrified over the past two decades with restored 19th century neoclassical homes, pedestrian streets, cafès, restaurants and tavernas which serve typical Greek specialties including moussaka, shish kebabs and souvlaki. Most visitors to Athens spend most of their time simply basking in the glory of the Acropolis from an alfresco table in the area and bypass the option of other attractions close by including the Ancient Agora and the changing of the guard at the Greek Parliament in Syntagma Square.

CHEFS AT SEA, ANTON MOSIMANN

Swiss-born Anton Mosimann is known throughout the world for his culinary expertise, has held many prestigious positions and received many accolades during his career. In 1985 he created 'cuisine naturelle', a healthy style of cooking with flavour, and in 1988 he opened his self-titled private dining club, in Belgravia, London. Today, very much a chef in demand, Mosimann travels the globe creating, cooking and masterminding events. He is a regular guest chef with Crystal Cruises, and on a cruise aboard the Crystal Serenity from Istanbul to Athens, he created some of his favourite dishes in a demonstration for guests, and spoke to us about his experiences of travelling and cooking at sea.

'Early in my career, I decided the only way forward for me was to work for the best chefs and in the best restaurants, so that led me to travel a lot at a young age. Today, everywhere I go in the world, I always make sure I check out the local market to see what produce is fresh. This is the best way to get a feel for the food and the culture of a place, and the market will give you inspiration on how to prepare and cook food in that particular part of the world. Cooking is all about timing, so when I am cooking at a venue, wherever it is, the first question I always ask is how far the kitchen is from the dining room. This is because my food doesn't travel. It is meant to be cooked and eaten right away. On cruise ships, therefore, that can be a big challenge. Another challenge is cooking when there is motion! On board today's top cruise ships, the standards are very high, the kitchens are fantastic to work in, and the chefs are extremely professional. Compared to cooking in a restaurant, one of the differences I notice is that you see 400 people sit down to dinner all at once, and an hour later they leave, but it's always well organised. When you cook for a large number of people like that, it's all about planning. I plan the food according to the venue, the location and the part of the world you're in. But yes, sometimes that's quite a challenge.'

CARRY ON COUSCOUS

In recent years, the cuisines of North Africa and the Middle East have become more popular, and a staple part of both diets is couscous, a tiny pasta made from rolled, dried semolina. Most people who prepare couscous at home use a processed, easy-to-cook variety sold in supermarkets, which takes couscous from the stove top or microwave to the table in a matter of minutes. But few people realise that the preparation of traditional couscous was labour intensive, almost ritual, involving considerable effort in both the milling and the cooking stages. Groups of women would gather together and work as a team for several days, making large batches which could be used over a period of months. To make the couscous, the women took semolina, sprinkled it with water, and rolled it by hand to form small pellets. These pellets are then sprinkled with dry flour to keep them separate, and then they are sieved. The pellets which are too small pass through the sieve are sprinkled with dry semolina and rolled again, and this process continues until all of the semolina has been transformed into tiny grains of couscous. The batches of couscous are then dried in the sun.

When properly cooked, couscous should be light and fluffy, and many chefs cite the traditional cooking process as the only way to truly achieve this, and for the uninitiated, it's equally as labour intensive as the milling; it is steamed two or even three times, sometimes over several days, in a large pot until the correct texture is achieved. Today, couscous is a flexible food which is served in a variety of ways, including with vegetables, meat, fish or seafood. In some countries it is served in broths and stews, and in Tunisia there's a sweet version of couscous, which has nuts, dates and spices and is eaten for breakfast. In France, couscous has become so popular that it's considered a national dish, and in the USA, it is referred to as a type of pasta. But one common couscous dish most people will have heard of and tried is taboule or tabouleh; a salad of Lebanese origins in which the couscous is mixed with olive oil, chopped tomatoes, onion, mint, parsley, salt and pepper, then chilled.

Cocktails

Bacarazz Martini
(Created by Nathan, a bartender on the Crystal Serenity)

1 part Bacardi Raspberry
1 part cranberry juice
7-8 fresh raspberries

Mash all of the raspberries, saving two for garnish, and press through a sieve. Then put the raspberries, Bacardi and cranberry juice into a cocktail shaker with ice and shake. Strain into a small martini glass, garnish with the remaining two raspberries, and serve.

Blue Aegean

1 part vodka
1 part Blue Curacao
3 parts fresh orange juice
A dash of soda water

Fill a tall glass with ice, add the vodka, Blue Curacao and orange juice and stir. Top up with a dash of soda water, and serve.

LEFT: Bacarazz Martini

Recipes

Grilled Scallops with Vegetable Ragout

(Supplied by chef Anton Mosimann)

16 fresh scallops (in shell)
Olive oil
Salt and freshly ground pepper
A few small sprigs of fresh basil to garnish
1 small zucchini, cut in half lengthwise and seeded
1 small yellow zucchini, cut in half lengthwise and seeded
1 small red capsicum, seeded
1 small yellow capsicum, seeded
1 small green capsicum, seeded
1 small eggplant (aubergine)
4 tbsp olive oil
3 medium tomatoes, skinned, seeded and diced
1 garlic clove, peeled and crushed
4 fresh basil leaves, finely shredded

Open the scallops with the tip of a small strong knife, then scoop them off the half shell with a soup spoon. Remove the debris and wash briefly but thoroughly to remove all the grit. Rim and pat dry, then brush the scallops with olive oil and season lightly. Set aside in a cool place until needed.

To make the ragout, dice all the vegetables, then heat the olive oil in a pan and sauté with the diced tomato and garlic for a few minutes. Season with salt and pepper and add the shredded basil. Keep hot or allow to cool as the ragout can be served hot or cold.

Preheat the grill to high, and grill the scallops for 20 seconds on each side. To serve, arrange the scallops on a bed of the vegetable ragout and garnish with basil.

Serves four

Grilled Seabass with Octopus & Garlic Couscous

4 fillets of seabass
4 baby octopus
1 cup red wine
¼ cup of balsamic vinegar
1 tsp of harissa
1½ cups couscous
4 tbsp butter or margarine
4 garlic cloves, crushed
1 litre (2 pints) chicken stock
rosemary to garnish

In a saucepan, bring half of the stock to the boil, add the octopus and simmer gently until tender. Drain and cool. Mix the red wine, balsamic vinegar and harissa together, pour over the cooked octopus and stand for at least three hours (preferably overnight in the fridge).

Put the couscous in a large bowl, boil the remaining stock and pour it over the couscous. Cover tightly with plastic wrap, and allow to stand until all of the liquid is absorbed. In a saucepan, melt the butter or margarine over a gentle heat, add garlic and sauté for a few minutes until the garlic is soft. Add the couscous to the pan and stir for about 2–3 minutes.

Pan fry the sea bass over a medium heat until fully cooked. At the same time, add a little olive oil to a frying pan and sear the octopus in the olive oil until crispy. To serve, place a small mound of the couscous on each plate, then place a piece of sea bass on top of the couscous. Top the fish with a baby octopus, and garnish with a sprig of rosemary. Serve with your choice of green vegetables such as French beans or snowpeas.

Serves four

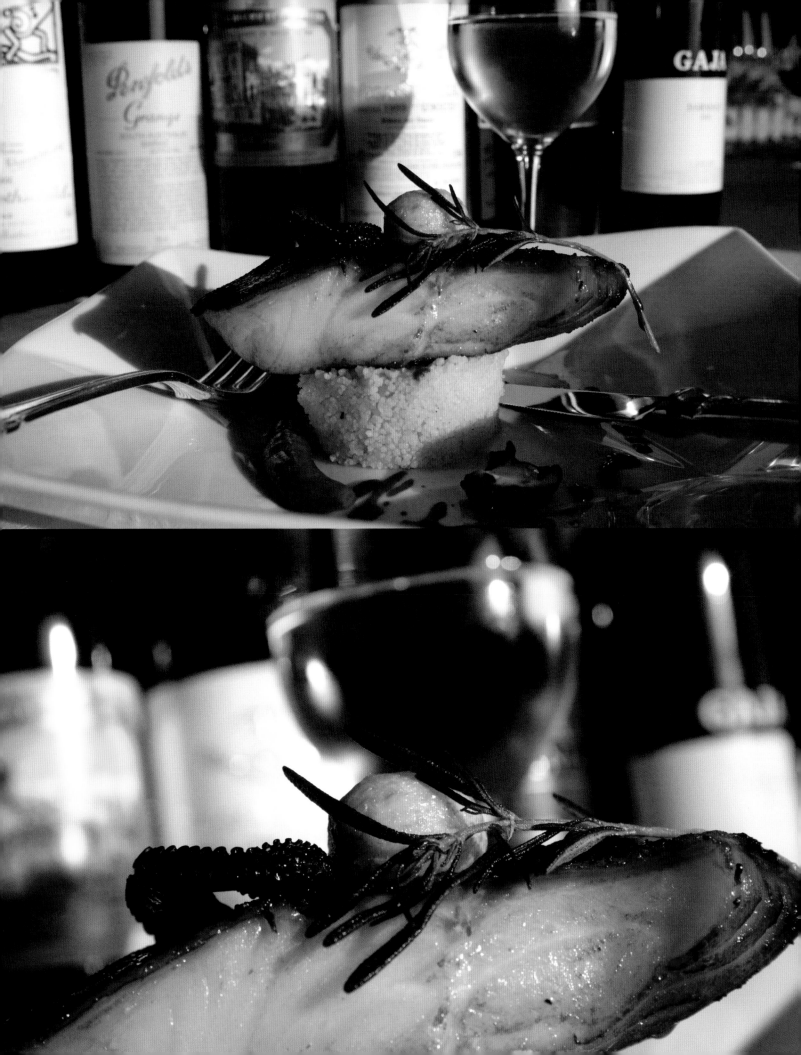

Stuffed Vine Leaves (Dolmades) with Tzatziki

450g (1lb) ground beef
1 medium yellow onion, minced
dried oregano
fresh parsley, finely chopped
mint leaves, cut into long, thin strips
2/3 cup rice, uncooked
salt and freshly ground black pepper
450g (16oz) or ½ kg of vine leaves
1 litre (2 pints) of chicken or vegetable stock

For the tzatziki
1 cucumber, peeled, deseeded and coarsely grated
200ml (7fl oz) Greek yoghurt
4 garlic cloves, crushed
handful of freshly chopped mint
juice of ½ a lemon
extra virgin olive oil (optional)

In a bowl mix the raw ground beef, onion, oregano, parsley, mint, rice, salt, and pepper. Carefully separate the vine leaves, and place on a wooden board shiny side down (stem towards you). Put a teaspoon of the meat stuffing near the bottom of each leaf, fold the bottom and 2 sides to cover the filling, and roll tightly toward the tip of the leaf. Place the rolled leaves in a casserole dish or pan, cover with several of the remaining leaves, and cover completely with stock or water. Cook in the oven at 175°C (350°F) for approximately 1 hour, making sure that the rice and the leaves are tender and all the stock is absorbed. Remove from oven and allow to cool.

To make the tzatziki, mix all of the ingredients together into a bowl and mix. To serve as a a meze, place the dolmades on a plate with pieces of fetta cheese, kalamata olives, the tzatziki, sun-dried tomatoes or peppers, and crackers or pieces of toasted pitta bread.

Makes approximately 50 dolmades

Turkish Delight

1 ltr (1¾ pints) water
900g (2lb) sugar
285g (10oz) corn flour
225g (8oz) icing sugar
1½ tbsp rosewater
2 tsp lemon juice
1 tsp cream of tartar
red food colouring (optional)

Place the sugar, a quarter of the water, and the lemon juice in a saucepan on a medium heat, and stir until the sugar dissolves and the mixture boils. Reduce the heat and simmer gently, without stirring, until the mixture forms a soft ball which can be squashed flat. Then remove the saucepan from the heat.

In a second saucepan, mix 225g (8oz) of the cornflour and the cream of tartar on a medium heat, and gradually stir in the remaining water until no lumps remain. continue stirring until the mixture boils and forms a thick paste, then slowly add the hot sugar syrup. Reduce the heat and simmer, stirring frequently to prevent sticking, for about 1 hour, or until the mixture has become a pale golden colour. Stir in the rosewater and add food colouring if used (if you want to make other colours separate the mixture into batches, and add a colour to each one).

Pour the mixture into a baking tin, spread evenly, cool to room temperature, and allow to stand overnight to set. Once set, sift the icing sugar and a little cornflour onto a cutting board, then turn the Turkish Delight out of the tin and cut it into squares with an oiled knife. Roll pieces in the icing sugar mixture to coat well.

Makes approximately 80 pieces

Mediterranean/Western Me

03:
Western Mediterranean

*S*teeped in history and rich traditions, it's possible to follow in the footsteps of the great artists, poets and conquerors in the Western Mediterranean, a romantic region which is a heady mix of European cultures and some of the most important and beautiful architecture in the world.

From the grandeur of Florence to the glitz and glamour of Monte Carlo, cruising the region is as much about history and culture as it is martinis and maseratis. This is where you can go wine tasting in the Tuscan Hills, sip espresso at a stand-up bar in the birthplace of the Renaissance, walk Monaco's famous Grand Prix circuit, wander through the cobbled alleys of medieval towns on the way to a day at the beach, or just sit back on deck and watch as the stunning coastline of the French Riviera passes by. The Western Mediterranean possesses a myriad of unique experiences which define the essence of the region, both on the mainland and the islands.

Italy, France, Monaco and Spain are the major destinations for cruises in the Western Mediterranean and the cuisine of the countries ranges from rustic to sophisticated, and gastronomes delight in the passion which accompanies even the most simple meals. It's this tradition which draws many people in, perhaps as much as the beautiful landscapes and wonderful architecture.

Monaco

It's one of those classic blue-sky days the Côte d'Azur is renowned for, and as the ship approaches Cap Ferrat she slows and bears starboard. We're ahead of schedule and cruise at a very leisurely speed along one of the most famous coastlines in the world.

Perched along the rugged cliffs are mansions, grand villas and historic hotels which bounce the bright sunlight back across the water. It's time to don the designer shades, order a glass of champagne, and be a part of the French Riviera party set, even if just for a day or two.

Before long we're cruising past the Musée Océanographique, perched dramatically on a cliff, and then the grandeur of Monaco reveals itself, bathed in sunshine with the casino as its heart, and arcing gracefully down the steep slope to its beautiful harbour.

Magnificent yachts of multimillionaires and billionaires jostle for supremacy along the harbour front and the cruise ship docks on the edge of the flotilla, towering above and commanding 360 degree views of the surreal city skyline.

It's the playground of the mega-rich and famous, but down at street level Monaco is refined, unpretentious and a joy to discover. First impressions are that it looks as though Manhattan or Hong Kong cruised past and tried to squeeze itself into the tiny 1.2 square kilometres (¾ mile) that Monaco sits on right up against the Côte d'Azure.

ABOVE: Musée Océanographique, Monte Carlo

The Principality of Monaco is the second smallest independent state in the world (after the Vatican) and is the epitome of wealth and glamour. Ferraris, Rolexes and designer clothes are commonplace, as are multi-million dollar yachts manned by private staff. This is how the 'other half' lives and it's unashamedly unconcerned by its outward ostentatiousness. On the surface, Monaco and its main city, Monte Carlo, appear to be a very exclusive club, and many people feel that at any stage they're likely to get tapped on the shoulder and be asked to leave.

But the reality is that as long as you dress well, the local Monégasques are happy to share their city with visitors and are nowhere near as snooty or dismissive as you'd expect. It is a playground for the rich and famous, and it's quite okay to go and have a look. It's a city that's famous for the annual Formula One Grand Prix and its casino but there's more to Monaco than those two icons and the only way to get around is on foot. Because the principality is basically cut into a very steep mountainside, there is some trekking involved and there are seven public escalators and elevators which make the exploration easier.

Every day at 11.55am, the Palais Princier (Prince's Palace) in old Monaco-Ville has a changing of the guard which provides a bit of colour and movement. West of Monte Carlo, this is where the Royal Family resides and the palace is on top of an area simply called The Rock. First built in the 13th century, it has been added to and enhanced over the centuries. Guided tours of the Palace run most of the day, and this is a great spot to take in the magnificent view of Monte Carlo Harbour on one side and the Mediterranean and the newer harbour district of Fontvieille on the other. The Rock is an old fortified town and within a few hundred metres of each other there are also restaurants and shops, a Cathedral, City Hall, and museums including the Musée Océanographique, which commands majestic views of the Mediterranean.

Inaugurated in 1910 by Monaco's modernist reformer Prince Albert I, the impressive building took 11 years to build and used 100,000 tonnes of stone. For those lucky enough to sail into Monaco, the Museum is the first thing most people see from the ocean. Inside the museum features a remarkable collection of sea life including seahorses, turtles, jellyfish, sharks, rays, lobsters, crabs, eels, urchins and sea animal skeletons. There's also maritime objects such as model ships, tools and weapons used in warfare. In all there are more than 4,000 different fish and 200 families of invertebrates.

Perhaps the most famous of all the tourist attractions in Monaco is the casino which is located in one of the most beautiful parts of Monte Carlo. Entry into the Casino is 10Euro and a strict dress code of jacket and tie is enforced for men, but the cost of entry is worth it just to marvel at the architecture inside which includes lavish marble and golden ornaments, stained glass windows, paintings and sculptures. Access to other gaming rooms also incurs additional costs and it's here that you'll find stern looking men gambling in near silence with thousands of dollars as a minimum, and the smell of expensive cognac and cigars hanging in the air.

This is the snapshot of decadence that sums up the essence of Monaco and it's a surreal and fun way to become a part of the Monte Carlo set, even if it's just for a day or two.

THE ART OF THE BARISTA

Coffee is one of the most consumed beverages in the world, and the history of its discovery and development is an intricate web of chance events, political intrigue, and the pursuit of wealth and power. Although records indicate that Arab traders were the first to bring coffee beans back to their homeland to boil and drink in around 1000AD, when it comes to Western Europe, it took a bit more time for coffee to get a secure foothold in day-to-day society. In Italy, the first coffeehouse is said to have opened in 1645, and in Paris the same historic day was almost thirty years later in 1672. Fast-forward to 1971, however, and the opening of the first Starbuck's in Seattle's Pike Place market caused a veritable public frenzy over fresh-roasted whole bean coffee.

In the past 30 years, coffee has become a daily ritual in the lives of many people. Every morning, millions of devotees across the globe awake with a single question on their lips: how good will my coffee be today? Creating the perfect coffee is the responsibility of a barista, or a professional coffee maker. The name 'barista' has its origins in Italy, and it's a title which isn't easily earned. Similar to a professional bartender, a barista is a highly trained individual who has a thorough understanding of how to work with coffee, and specialises in making drinks from almost any incarnation of the coffee bean. To become one you have a lot more to learn than just making drinks; to become a top barista you need to know the history of coffee, as well as the process it undergoes before it arrives in your cup. The skill of the barista can make the difference between happy and dissatisfied customers, so ultimately there's a lot riding on his or her shoulders. A true barista is one that learns everything there is to know about coffee because they love everything about it.

Florence

It dominates the skyline of Florence, standing sentinel over the city that gave birth to the Renaissance. The Campanile's 414 steps end with one of the most distinctive panoramas in Europe. The climb itself is a challenging exercise, and the higher up the stone staircase, the more steep and confined the ascent becomes. Most people who attempt the 84 metre (91 yard) climb up the gothic bell tower admit they wonder if it's all going to be worth it but the physical exertion is rewarded on the final platform at the top. It's a 360 degree panorama of red roofs, church spires and the piazzas of Florence, while in the distance the Tuscan hills frame the scene. Down below, horse-drawn carriages clip-clop along the cobbled streets and artists set up displays in the piazza ahead of the expected influx of visitors later in the morning.

But the real glory of this hard-earned vista is the Cathedral of Santa Maria del Fiore, known locally as *il Duomo*, because of Filippo Brunelleschi's cupola which crowns the magnificent building. In a city that's crammed full of fantastic churches, monasteries, palaces, museums and towers, this is the epicentre of the birthplace of the Italian Renaissance and it inspires and uplifts not just art lovers, but even the most stubborn philistines. The Duomo itself is an important symbol of the Renaissance and not just a stunning landmark. Brunelleschi's cupola was an ingenious engineering feat which required unique methods and equipment which transformed the way building design was carried out. His methods were used in many of Europe's famous domes, including St. Peters in Rome. Its importance to the people of Florence is also summed up by the locals' phrase for being homesick—*nostalgia del cupolone*—which literally means 'homesick for the dome'. In Florence, the Duomo and the Campanile are merely the starting points of an exploration of a city which reveals one surprise after another in a place that really hasn't changed much since the 16th century.

Tucked in just behind the Duomo is the Battistero, or Baptistry, which is one of Florence's oldest structures with foundations that date back to the 4th and 5th centuries. Its ornate doors make this one of the special sights of Florence and one man, Lorenzo Ghiberti, spent most of his adult life from 1403–52 making these vast structures. The originals have been removed and stored to prevent damage from pollution, but the copies that have replaced them are no less impressive. Walking Florence's cobbled streets takes you in the footsteps of the likes of Michelangelo, Dante and Botticelli and it seems that at at every turn there's a piazza or square with famous statues and sophisticated cafés to sit down, have a real espresso, and take it all in. The most famous square is the Piazza della Signoria which has been the civic centre of Florence since it was built around the end of the 13th century. It's dominated by the 14th century Palazzo della Signoria and has a swag of other important buildings around it including the Uffizi Gallery, the Loggia della Signoria, the Palazzo degli Uguccioni and the Palazzo del Tribunale de Mercanzia.

Justifiably, the Uffizi Gallery is considered one of the best in Europe with an unmatched collection of Renaissance paintings and sculptures including works by Michelangelo, Sandro Botticelli, Rembrandt, Raphael, Titian and Caravaggio.

The museum occupies the top floor of the Palazzo degli Uffizi, which is right on the Arno River, and queues begin forming at the Uffizi from well before its 8.30am opening time. It's not uncommon to wait several hours to simply enter the museum but it is possible to reserve tickets by telephone in advance at an extra cost to beat the crowds.

Perhaps the most enduring image of Florence is the Ponte Vecchio, or Old Bridge, which has spanned the Arno River since the 14th century. It was also the only bridge in Florence that escaped destruction in WWII. Originally, this is where butchers, grocers and blacksmiths plied their trade but in 1593 the Medici grand duke Ferdinand I ordered these traders off the bridge. His private corridor which linked his palace to his office in the Uffizi crossed over the top of the shops. He wanted the plebeian rabble out and allowed goldsmiths in, and they remain there until this day. The anarchical structure now houses jewellery and souvenir shops which are geared towards the hordes of tourists that cross every day. A little further down river, the Basilica di Santa Croce (Basilica of the Holy Cross) is one of the finest examples of Italian Gothic architecture, with the possible exception of the Campanile, and the principal Franciscan church in Florence is also the home of some of the original Renaissance artwork and is the burial site for some of the golden age's famous figures.

Michelangelo's tomb is right inside and legend has it that he nominated that spot so that on Judgment Day when the graves of the dead open up, the first thing he would see would be the Duomo through the church doors. Galileo Galilei's tomb is also inside, along with that of Niccolo Machiavelli and Ghiberti, and standing among the tombs of some of the most influential 'minds' in history is a humbling, yet uplifting experience which sums up one of the truly important historical cities in the world.

SUPER TUSCANS

The name doesn't refer to a sports team or a rock and roll band, but a group of unusual Italian red wines from the Chianti wine growing region in Tuscany which have caused somewhat of a controversy. In fact, the rise of the Super Tuscans is one of the oddest and perhaps most revolutionary aspects of wine production over the last forty years. These blended red wines are technically unofficial, as they are not recognised by any of the Italian wine classification systems. The story of their evolution begins with the downturn in popularity and quality of Chianti in the 1970s. Chianti is a robust red wine made from a blend of grapes, predominantly Sangiovese. But when quality and consistency started to waver, a group of winemakers from the Chianti region deviated from the recognised regulations in a bid to produce better wines.

The result was the creation of some top quality new blends, but as the winemakers were not allowed to use the name Chianti on their wine labels due to the regulations, their efforts were classified as 'vino de tavola', or table wines, the lowest of all Italian wine qualities. The first Super Tuscan wine was released in 1978, and as others started to hit the market, prices for these so-called unofficial wines were soon higher than even the most well-known Chianti. Since the Super Tuscans were first produced, the rules have changed. Some producers have brought their wines back into the realm of the regulations, and others have not. One thing is for certain, if you refer to a Super Tuscan today, you are speaking of a wine with flair, flamboyance and power, with the flavour of new oak.

Corsica

From walking in the footsteps of the artists and poets of the Renaissance, to the birthplace of one of Europe's great conquerors, Corsica is a beautiful island which pays homage to its most famous former inhabitant, Napoleon Bonaparte. The fact that Napoleon never returned to his island home of Corsica once he left in 1779 to study at a French military school at the age of nine is seldom mentioned in this part of the world, although many will proudly claim to be descendants. Much of Corsica's claim to fame rests on its historical past, but the simple fact is that it's one of the most beautiful Mediterranean islands, with a unique landscape of high mountain ranges of pink, green and white granite, lined with lush forests. Add to that sheer cliffs that drop straight into the ocean, stunning beaches and idyllic villages that have changed little for hundreds of years and you end up with one of Europe's most unspoiled sanctuaries.

AJACCIO

Though distinctly French in flavour, its strategic location 168km south of Monaco and 81km (50 miles) west of Italy made Corsica and its capital Ajaccio a prize possession among Mediterranean powers, and much of the architecture is Italian with impressive citadels, bridges and churches. The island's motto is 'always conquered, never subdued' and that spirit of defiance remains with the locals who are happy to be French, but are staunchly Corsican at heart. Ajaccio, on the west coast of Corsica, is encircled by wood-covered mountains to the rear of the town, and sits on the port guarded by its ancient citadel on the Gulf of Ajaccio. Although technically a city, Ajaccio itself is really just a large village, and it's possible to walk its elegant streets and take in the sights in half a day, even while stopping now and then at a café or restaurant to join in with the laid-back approach to life here.

The spectacular food market at Place Campinchi across the quai from the ferry port is a great place to start exploring with its exotic display of cheeses, pastries, sausages and local fish including the prehistoric rascasse (red scorpion fish). Place Foch and its Bonaparte statue is something of a central point for the Old Town with its typically Mediterranean houses, and wandering these narrow crooked streets is one of the highlights of Ajaccio, apart from 'conqueror spotting'. The Maison Bonaparte is now a national museum and is open to the public and it provides a fascinating insight into Corsica's most famous family. They moved into the house in 1682 and Napoleon was born here in 1769. It's an intimate experience with family furniture and photographs, various weapons and official documents, and Napoleon's mother's bedroom has been restored to what's believed to be its original condition.

For art and history lovers, however, the Musée Fesch would rank as one of the highlights with a fine collection of Italian masters from the likes of Botticelli and Canaletto. In all there are around 30,000 paintings that were 'acquired' by Napoleon's uncle, Cardinal Fesch, who was archbishop of Lyon when the French Revolution took place. Despite the fact that Ajaccio has beautiful architecture and museums, a friendly café culture and a nice white sand beach, it's not the only place on the island and there are many beautiful spots on Corsica. The best way to get around is by rental car, as public transport is quite poor. The island has many little villages to discover and many beautiful sites such as Bonifacio, Solenzara, Sarténe, Porto-Vecchio, Piana and Porto, and in between there's an endless number of great beaches and stunning lookouts over the Mediterranean. Slightly inland, the tiny village of Ota is made up of traditional stone houses that are cut into a steep mountain with a dramatic range as a backdrop.

Corsica has a mesmerising effect, especially on first-time visitors who often make the mistake of trying to do it all in one day from walking in the footsteps of Napoleon on the old streets of Ajaccio, to hiking the trails and swimming in the deep blue of the Mediterranean, but it's best to adopt the local attitude of slowing down and taking the time to enjoy a truly unique island.

Marseille

As the early morning sun rises above the Notre Dame de la Garde which towers over Marseille, the *Quai de Belges* is bathed in warm sunshine, sparking the fishermen into action. They haul crates of seafood, caught overnight, from their boats moored nearby and set them out on tables as their female partners (literally the fishwives) call out to the shoppers who flock to the colourful market each morning. Within half an hour the quai is bathed in bright sunlight and packed with locals, and above the hubbub of the busy market is a female voice with a beautiful rendition of Édith Piaf's *Non, je ne regrette rien* (No Regrets). The music hangs perfectly over the setting with Marseille's Vieux Port as a backdrop, and its source is a 72-year-old crooner called Fanny who's serenading passers-by with her Piaf covers.

As buskers go, Fanny not only remains faithful to the original version, but she also knows how to work the crowd. She calls out the younger men in the crowd to join her show which pretty much consists of holding their hand and singing soulfully while looking deep into their eyes. Fanny clearly enjoys the embarrassment she causes her 'victims', and even the sleep-deprived fishermen are forced into a grin at least. It's a warm welcome to a port city with a bit of a reputation as being a rough-and-gruff type of place. Marseille is a world away from the Provence portrayed in travel shows and absolutely nothing like the glitz and glamour of the Riviera, but it's a working city with real people and a genuine charm which surprises many visitors. The film *The French Connection* in the 1970s, which starred Gene Hackman, portrayed Marseille as a sleazy and dangerous gangster town, but these days the inner city suburbs and port area have been restored to provide a unique French experience.

The city is France's oldest and was founded more than 2,000 years ago by the Greeks from the city of Phocea. Ever since it's been a gateway for immigrants from Italy, Greece, Turkey and North Africa. Today, it's a dynamic multicultural city of just under one million people and the Vieux Port (or Old Port) is the heart and soul of Marseille, as it has been for centuries. It's a well protected U-shaped bay with the old fortresses of St Jean and St Nicholas at its entrance which now welcomes mostly pleasure craft and smaller fishing boats. Trestle tables line the harbour front, laden with an exotic mix of seafood and the nearby quays and arcades are lined with restaurants and cafés filled with locals who seem totally content to relax and watch the harbour life unfold in front of them.

Despite its colourful history, Marseille has little Greek or Roman architecture still standing, but the more modern monuments capture the brashness of France's second city. Towering above the city is the immense Notre Dame de la Garde, a Byzantine monument erected between 1853 and 1864 on the city's highest hill. The domed Basilica can be seen from pretty much everywhere in Marseille and its bell tower is topped by a 10 metre (30ft) tall gilded statue of the Virgin Mary on a 12 metre (40ft) high pedestal. Bullet holes mark the cathedral's outer walls as evidence of the fierce fighting that took place during the city's Battle of Liberation in 1944.

Ornate architecture and fascinating history aside, this is a great place to gain an orientation of the sprawling city with its 360 degree views, with the Vieux Port below and the terracotta roofs which stretch into the distance. The Abbaye St-Victor is halfway up the same hill as the Notre Dame de la Garde and the 12th century Romanesque building houses the tombs of third and fourth century martyrs including those of St Cassien and St Victor himself, who apparently was ground to death between millstones by the Romans.

Back down at sea level the Marseille Ferry Boat chugs back and forth across the Vieux Port. For a few coins you can cross from one side to the other and on the northern side the Hotel de Ville marks the hop-on-hop-off point, which also leads to the city's most fascinating suburb, Le Panier. The name literally translates as 'the Breadbasket' and the area is a complex maze of unmapped streets set on a hill—walking Le Panier may leave you confused about which side of the Mediterranean you're on. This is where many of the city's immigrants congregated when they arrived from North Africa and even today market traders are more likely to call out in Arabic than in French.

During WWII it was also a hideout for many Resistance fighters and Jewish people and although the German military razed the area many times, enough of it still remains to offer an authentic glimpse of Marseille's oldest quarter. Like the rest of Marseille, Le Panier has no airs and graces and asks nothing of its visitors other than to give it a fair go, and if you dig deep enough you'll find a slice of unique French culture with an eastern European and North African flavour.

ABOVE: Vieux Port, Marseille

UNIQUE SPECIALTIES OF MARSEILLE

As France's largest port city, and main point of entry into the country, culturally it has become a cosmopolitan melting pot and when it comes to cuisine, the city is known for many unique local delicacies. Some of these dishes draw influence from the cultural ethnic diversity of the city, while others take advantage of the city's Mediterranean location. Top of the list of Marseille favourites is bouillabaisse, a rich and hearty fish soup containing assorted shellfish, fish and vegetables, served with toasted bread and grated cheese. Another favourite is bourride, a fish dish made with monkfish, mayonnaise and a vegetable brunoise, a garnish of diced vegetables which have been blanched briefly in salty boiling water, then dipped in ice for a few seconds to set their colour. Marseille is also famous for a garlic sauce called aïoli, which is made from raw garlic, lemon juice, eggs and olive oil. It is traditionally served with boiled fish, hard boiled eggs and cooked vegetables. There's also tapenade, a paste made from capers, chopped olives and olive oil, and a close relative is anchoïade, a paste made from anchovies, garlic, black olives and olive oil.

THE BALEARIC ISLANDS

Just off the east coast of mainland Spain, the Balearics is an archipelago with four major islands which are undergoing something of a renaissance with the main destinations, Mallorca and Ibiza, shedding their reputations as a cheap getaway for package-deal Brits and Germans. Now people are catching onto the fact that they're polished and sophisticated places, and while the islands of Menorca and Formentera remain relatively quiet in comparison, Mallorca and Ibiza both have an Old Town, which are elegant with winding cobbled streets, loads of great cafés and original 17th century architecture. In fact, Ibiza Town's medieval city, Dalt Vila, was declared a UNESCO World Heritage Site in 1999.

Palma Cathedral, also known by its proper name La Seu, is the symbol of the island of Mallorca which is the largest of the Spanish Balearic islands in the Mediterranean. Beautiful inside with a sense of spaciousness, it's even more stunning seen from outside and the magnificent Gothic Cathedral appears to rise up out of the sea to stand out against the backdrop of the striking Sierra de Tramuntana mountain range. Such imposing beauty doesn't just get 'knocked up' in a year or two. This Cathedral took nearly 400 years to build from 1230 to 1600 and is under constant renovation and restoration.

LLEGEND AND READING

LEFT: Cruising Mallorca's coastline
BELOW: Interior of Palma Cathedral, Palma de Mallorca

For an island with a reputation as a package-deal beach holiday destination for European tourists, Mallorca and its capital city Palma in particular have a lot of important architectural monuments which confirm their rich history. Very few of the 20 million or so annual visitors to Mallorca bother to move from their high-rise-on-the-beach to take a closer look at the heart and soul of the island, and that's probably a good thing. It means on most days there's relatively little tourist traffic at the main sights like the Cathedral or at the adjacent Palau De L'Almudaina, a Muslim castle converted into a residence for the Mallorcan monarchs at the end of the 13th century.

Both Mallorca, and especially the city of Palma, and Ibiza have been rejuvenated and they're both now something of a style centre in the middle of the Mediterranean. They enjoy a wonderful climate, magnificent architecture, great nightlife, inexpensive and authentic Spanish food, and it's all wrapped up in languid Mediterranean style where doing very little, quite slowly, is perfectly acceptable.

Walking the city is the best way to get around and it helps provide the sense that café life is important to the local people. On a Sunday just before lunch time it's difficult to work out whether many of the people have actually been to, or are going to church, but they're decked out in their Sunday best, including the children. While parents kick back and enjoy the sunshine over an espresso and the papers, their children kick footballs around the cozy squares that seem to spring up at the end of every street.

And wandering the cobbled and winding streets of the medieval Old Towns is a relaxed way to disappear from the real world, even if for just a few hours.

MALÁGA & ANDALUCIA

Mainland Spain has around a half dozen cruise ports which feature on Western Mediterranean itineraries including Barcelona, Valencia, Almeria, Alicante and Cartagena, and thanks to a recent major redevelopment the Port of Malága has become the major base for cruises in the region. Located on the southern coast of Spain on the Costa del Sol, Malága is the capital of the region. It's a pretty and authentic Spanish city and its location right in the heart of Andalucia, a region which typifies what most people expect from Spain, makes it one of the most popular ports in the Western Mediterranean.

In Andalucia, you'll find remote white mountain villages, high sierras, bullfighting, flamenco and gypsies, and of course, if you so desire, long stretches of beach with all the trappings of mass tourism.

This is a typical day in Andalucia: you're driving through a tiny village with traditional white walled cottages and you brake as a goat herder leads his flock across the road. The goat herder, and his goats of course, are in no real hurry and nearby is a bar simply called *Miguel's*. It's an omen. You turn the engine off, wander in and grab an outside table to watch a bit of village life. It might be too early for a drink but the locals don't seem to care, so a beer it is. The local men, as they tend to do in this part of the world, congregate outside the church in the main square to chat and smoke cigarettes, and a wayward donkey is rounded up casually by its owner and led away. It's easy to become sidetracked by such diversions in Andalucia and it doesn't take long for the chill factor to kick in.

LEFT: Alhama Village, Andalucia
BELOW: La Herradura Beach, Andalucia

Andalucia is home to one of Europe's most inspiring architectural wonders, the magnificent Alhambra Palace in the city of Granada. The Alhambra Palace dominates the skyline, and overlooks the bustling city with an austere presence. It's the finest example of Moorish architecture in the world and its scale is overwhelming. Even the Andalucians struggle to describe its grandeur and several days are not enough to fully explore its maze of palaces, fortresses, churches, gardens and plazas.

To understand the history of the Alhambra is to grasp the history of Andalucia itself. The Moors arrived in the region in 711AD and made Granada one of their strongholds. It's believed construction of the Alhambra in its current form began in 1238 under an Islamic dynasty and continued until 1492 when the Catholic Monarchs Ferdinand and Isabel conquered Granada. This naturally meant a change in architectural style. During the 18th and part of the 19th century it fell into disrepair until it was declared a national monument in 1870. At every turn within the fortressed walls of the Alhambra is a piece of history which typifies the Andalucian heart.

Just outside the Alhambra Palace walls is the Albaicin, a neighbourhood which is a maze of narrow streets, white walled homes and Moorish handicrafts and art laid out on street corners. However, it's the tapas bars which draw the locals into the area. Each drink is accompanied by a small plate of food, and this is a great way to sample some of the street culture. It doesn't take long to absorb the region's rich history, gastronomic delights and locally made wine and sherry, stunning mountain scenery, fabulous beaches and sheer natural beauty. It's no wonder Andalucians believe they've inherited a slice of heaven.

CUISINE AT SEA, LE CORDON BLEU

Over the years, food has become an integral part of the cruise experience. Forget any ideas of all-you-can-eat buffets and burgers. At the luxury end of the scale in particular, the quality and diversity of cuisine can be a major influence for discerning travellers when choosing to cruise on a particular ship. With this in mind, Regent Seven Seas Cruises and Le Cordon Bleu joined forces some years ago to establish exclusive restaurants, on Regent's two all-suite all-balcony ships, the Seven Seas Mariner and Seven Seas Voyager. Called Signatures, the restaurants are 'by reservation only' mirror images of each other, featuring a fixed à la carte menu of traditional French dishes, complemented by a menu of Cordon Bleu 'specials' which change frequently to embrace local and seasonal ingredients at each port of call.

The name *Le Cordon Bleu* has been synonymous with culinary excellence since the 16th century, but its reputation as a leader in the art of innovative cuisine has been internationally accepted since the establishment of its famed Parisian cooking school in 1895. Today, the organisation has more than 29 schools in five continents, and its elite tutoring attracts more than 20,000 students every year. On certain Regent cruises, Le Cordon Bleu takes its culinary expertise and training to the high seas. Cooking workshops are held, allowing small groups of guests the rare opportunity of taking instruction from a Le Cordon Bleu chef, with a theme based on a particular port of call. The guests are given cooking demonstrations, participate in hands-on classes, and at the end of the three-day course, they each receive a prized memento for their efforts, a Le Cordon Bleu Certificate of Attendance.

Cocktails

Sangria

5 parts Spanish red wine
1 part Cointreau
1 part brandy
1 part Bacardi
dash of sugar syrup
slices of orange, lime, lemon, and berries

Pour all ingredients in order into a jug, mix and garnish with the fruit.
Pour into a tall wine glass, and serve.

Kir Royale

½ part cognac
dash of Creme de Cassis
French Champagne

Pour Creme de Cassis and cognac into a flute glass and mix.
Add cold Champagne and serve.

LEFT: Sangria

Recipes

Spinach Stuffed Snails (Escargot)

2 dozen large canned snails (with shells) rinsed and drained
280g (10oz) of spinach
4 tbsp butter
1 tbsp minced garlic
1 tbsp of finely chopped shallots
1 tbsp of minced parsley
¼ tsp of salt
¼ tsp of freshly ground black pepper
¼ cup of Parmesan cheese, grated
¼ cup of wholemeal breadcrumbs
¼ cup of chicken stock
1 stick of French bread

Cook the spinach, drain, squeeze dry and chop finely in a blender. Then cook the snails according to the instructions. In a saucepan, melt a little of the butter over a medium heat, then add the garlic, shallots, parsley, salt and pepper and cook gently. Once the garlic and shallots are cooked, add the remaining butter, the cheese and the breadcrumbs and stir until the mixture is smooth and thick.

Take the snails, and remove the flesh from each one. Stuff each shell with a little of the mixture, then replace the snail flesh and fill out the shell with more mixture until full. Place the snails on a baking tray, and bake in the oven at 175°C (350°F) for about 15 minutes. Serve hot with slices of French bread. If you can't find snails with shells, you can stuff the snail and mixture into large pasta shells, or small mushrooms with the stalks removed.

Serves four

Penne with Basil & Chilli

500g (1lb) fresh penne pasta
2 small red chillies, finely chopped
½ cup of semi-sun dried tomatoes, chopped
4 cloves of fresh garlic, crushed
1 small red onion finely diced
½ cup of fresh basil, chopped
½ cup of chicken stock
2 tbsp extra virgin olive oil
Freshly ground black pepper
Parmesan cheese, grated

In a deep frying pan or skillet, combine the chillies, garlic, onion, stock, and olive oil, and cook over a medium heat for about 10 minutes. In a separate pan, cook the pasta in lightly salted water until al dente - tender but firm. Then drain the pasta and add to the frying pan, along with the semi-sun dried tomatoes, half of the chopped basil and pepper to taste. To serve, divide between four plates, sprinkle with the remaining basil and add Parmesan cheese if desired.

Serves four

Gaspacho Andaluz

(Supplied by chef Anton Mosimann)

600g (1¼lb) ripe tomatoes, skinned
1 green capsicum, seeded
1 red capsicum, seeded
1 small onion, peeled
½ garlic clove, peeled
½ cucumber, peeled
1 slice of fresh bread, crusts removed and made into breadcrumbs
1½ tbsp red wine vinegar
5 tbsp vegetable stock
4 tbsp olive oil
A few fresh oregano leaves
4 fresh basil leaves, shredded
Salt and freshly ground pepper
½ cup of croûtes

Chop the tomatoes, capsicums, onion, garlic and cucumber roughly, and mix with the breadcrumbs in a large bowl. Add the red wine vinegar, stock, olive oil and herbs, and season to taste with salt and pepper. Leave to marinate for 12 hours in the fridge. About 2–3 hours prior to serving, purée the mixture in small batches in a blender or food processor, then push through a sieve (alternatively, purée using a food mill). Pour the soup into a serving bowl, taste for seasoning and chill. When ready to serve, garnish the soup with croûtes, diced capsicums, cucumber and herbs, or simply sprinkle with strips of fresh basil.

Serves four

Corsican Cheesecake

2 lemons, grated zest only
6 large eggs
$^2/_3$ cup of sugar
2 tsp vanilla extract
900g (2lb) whole milk ricotta cheese
Icing sugar
Fresh fruit to garnish

Blanch the lemon zest in boiling water and plunge into cold water before draining well. Separate the eggs, and in a mixing bowl beat the egg yolks, sugar and vanilla extract using an electric mixer until thick and lemon coloured. Cream the ricotta cheese in a food processor until smooth, then gradually add it and the lemon zest into the egg yolk mixture and beat slowly until smooth. In a separate bowl, beat the egg whites until stiff, then add a third of it to the cheese mixture and whisk by hand. Then gently fold in the remaining egg whites until the mixture is well blended and no streaks of white remain.

Butter and flour a 22cm cheesecake dish or springform pan, and pour the mixture into it. Place in the centre of the oven and bake at 160°C (325°F) until the cheesecake is golden brown. Once cooked, transfer to a rack to cool and refrigerate. To serve, place a slice of the cheesecake on a plate, dust the top with icing sugar, and garnish with fresh fruit.

Serves six to eight

Cheese Soufflé

½ cup of grated Gruyere cheese
4 large eggs
1 cup of hot milk
4 tbsp of butter
3 tbsp flour
Salt, pepper and nutmeg to taste

In a pan, gently melt the butter then add the flour and stir. Gradually add the hot milk, and season with the salt, pepper and nutmeg. Remove the sauce from the heat, and blend in the egg yolks. Then beat the egg whites until they are stiff, and carefully fold into the egg yolk mixture.
Add grated cheese.

Butter a soufflé dish, pour the mixture into it and bake in a hot oven at 200°C (400°F) for about 20 minutes. Do not open the oven door while the soufflé is cooking as it will make it go flat. Serve immediately once cooked.

Serves four

04:
Asia

ver since Marco Polo returned from his epic 20-year exploration of Asia in the late 13th century, this vast and beautiful region has attracted travellers from around the world. Few places on earth offer such a diversity of sensory experiences. It's a blend of exotic cultures, imposing cityscapes, ancient temples and pagodas and bustling markets, all somehow fused together to form a complex and fascinating canvas.

To cruise Asia is to follow in the wake of ancient maritime traders and explorers where it's possible to sail into the majesty of Hong Kong Harbour, observe the centuries-old Saigon River life, explore the steamy craziness of Bangkok and Ho Chi Minh City, be overwhelmed by the rich history of China and glide past tranquil islands with tropical jungles. Most itineraries in the region focus on Hong Kong, Singapore and Thailand, and for good reason, but increasingly Vietnam, China, Japan, the Philippines and Taiwan are being added to increase the diversity of the ports-of-call even further.

The cuisine of the region is important to its people, and while the cooking styles and produce differ in each country and sub-region, the ritual of preparing and eating meals is paramount in family life.

China

The sheer size of mainland China and number of people within its borders have produced a diverse nation, which for centuries was one of the great civilisations. China bestowed an enduring legacy in the arts and sciences to the world and today is the dominant culture of Asia.

Asia is fast becoming one of the world's economic powerhouses, with rapid growth and rampant construction producing a new wave of wealth and millionaires in the big cities, although poverty remains a reality for people in the regional areas.

Spread over an area of 9.6 million square kilometres with a population approaching one and a half billion people, variations in language and customs are inevitable. Against this backdrop is the physical grandeur of China which can be seen in its vast countryside with villages, and its gleaming cities by the sea which offer a mind-boggling snapshot of where this country is heading.

The major ports of call include the capital city and China's cultural heart, Beijing, the country's biggest city and economic centre, Shanghai, and Hong Kong, the former British colony with its multiple personalities.

HONG KONG

As the ship reverses from Ocean Terminal into Victoria Harbour, scores of smaller boats approach to watch the amazing spectacle and hundreds of people head to the 'Avenue of the Stars' on the waterfront to see what all the fuss is about. The spectator craft, which includes harbour cruise operators, pleasure boats and traditional junks, surround the ship and for a while it looks as though her route out of Hong Kong may be delayed for quite some time. But the ship's captain issues three long blasts of the horn which reverberate around the harbour and bounce off the skyscrapers, and the flotilla beats a hasty retreat to a safe distance.

Any cruise which sails into, or out of, Hong Kong is a special event and it's easy to see why it's consistently rated the number one destination in the world by cruise passengers. With Hong Kong Island on one side and Kowloon on the other, this is one of the most stunning cityscapes in the world. Towering skyscrapers compete for supremacy and a few of them flicker alive with their neon facades as if to signal the onset of nightfall.

Thankfully, it takes time for the ship to negotiate its way out of Hong Kong and this allows the amazing spectacle to unfold. On the water below, all manner of boats, including the ubiquitous *Star Ferries*, criss-cross the harbour and try to dodge the ship as she heads out of the harbour at a very civilised speed. Behind us, the nightly 'Symphony of Lights' show in Victoria Harbour begins. The extravagant laser and music show across 44 landmark skyscrapers seems a fitting farewell for our journey along one of the great shipping routes. Soon the commercial buildings of the world's biggest corporations give way to the urban tower blocks which line the harbour front and more traditional junks putter out from their moorings to get a closer look at our overwhelming presence on the water.

RIGHT: A Chinese tailor works in a Hong Kong market
BELOW: Temple Street Night Market, Hong Kong

NEXT PAGE
Daily life Hong Kong style

Hong Kong has a powerful and unforgettable effect on the senses. Walk the streets in the shadows of its surreal skyline—a unique energy takes hold and you could be on the set of an epic drama in a city which is as inspiring and enchanting as it is overwhelming. From a ride on the *Star Ferry*, to the views of its spectacular skyscrapers from Victoria Peak, and its unstoppable market life, Hong Kong slows down for nobody. It's also a city where past and present fuse comfortably.

There are so many images for the first-timer, and return visitor, to take in: traditional wooden boats bobbing on the harbour next to ferries and luxury cruise ships; decayed buildings cowering next to glass and steel skyscrapers; tired alleys meandering behind luxury hotels; old Chinese traders with wheel barrows pushing past late model BMWs and Mercedes Benzes.

These contradictions help form Hong Kong's most striking characteristic. It's a merger of the old and the new, ancient and advanced with ultra-modern skyscrapers built using traditional bamboo scaffolding, and sophisticated restaurants with old-fashioned street stalls out front. At every turn, there's a flashback to a past era and a fast-forward to modern city living.

Hong Kong's western fabric was woven by the British; from the schools and free market economy, to the double decker buses and a pint of ale at the end of a working day, but its soul remains undoubtedly Chinese, from the lively street vendors to its Bhuddist temples to the traditional herbal medicine shops.

With seven million inhabitants living elbow-to-elbow in a territory of just 1100 sq km (60 sq miles), it's possible to suffer from sensory overload in a metropolis that's one big, visual spectacular.

SHANGHAI

For the sail-in to Shanghai, evidence of its emergence as one of the fastest growing cities in the world is literally all around us: cargo ships of all sizes form a two-lane maritime convoy of those delivering to the city, and those that have just picked up. Massive cranes work 24/7 to unload the seemingly endless amount of cargo that moves through Asia's biggest city which is now reportedly the world's busiest port, in terms of cargo tonnage.

With 16 million people, it's the largest city in the world's most populous country and at street level it has an energy that reflects its status as the economic, financial and commercial capital of China. While it lacks the architectural grandeur of China's more famous cities, the building boom is evident with the sheer number of cranes working to deliver more skyscrapers to a place that already has more than 3,000 of them.

The name Shanghai literally means 'city on the sea' although it actually sits on the Huangpu River, a tributary of the Yangtze which empties into the East China Sea. The river is the lifeblood of Shanghai and highlights why this is one of the world's great maritime cities with a steady stream of traffic along the waterway, including massive barges carting steel and concrete up river to feed the cranes that stretch into the distance. Not surprisingly, Shanghai is China's richest city and is regarded as a model for the future of the country with modern architecture, international restaurants, trendy bars, expansive shopping malls and late model European cars blending together to create a truly grand city to rival the likes of Hong Kong and Bangkok.

Shanghai's links to trade with the Western world at the turn of the 20th century mean it has an East-meets-West feel with some traditional Chinese architecture mixed in with French flair, and the occasional art-deco building which wouldn't be out of place in New York or Chicago.

Singapore

It has an international reputation as a shoppers' paradise, and when Singaporeans tell you shopping is a sport in their country, they're not joking. Modern air-conditioned shopping malls and traditional markets are literally everywhere with sales promising plenty of savings. The Singapore experience is very much a 'soft landing' into Asia.

From the efficient underground train system, the Mass Rapid Transit or MRT, regulated and inexpensive taxis, to its tree-lined streets and overall cleanliness for a busy city (there really is no litter anywhere), it is the model of efficiency which has earned it the nickname 'the Switzerland of Asia'. But that's not to say it lacks charm and diversity. In one day it's possible to sit down to a meal of Peking Duck in Chinatown, sweat through an authentic curry at Little India, listen to the Call to Prayer on Arab Street, go shopping for designer label clothing on Orchard Road, and sip tea on starched linen table cloths at the colonial era icon, the Raffles Hotel.

It's very much an easy place to explore and most cruise ships dock at the Singapore Cruise Centre in Keppel Harbour, which has an MRT station that allows easy access to most of the city. It's also a 15 minute taxi ride to the major city sights.

Singapore's history as a mosquito-ridden swamp occupied by opium addicts and ne'er-do-wells seems an impossibility amid the techno-dazzle of modern day Singapore. It was founded by a Sumatran dynasty in the 13th century, and its fortunes changed dramatically in 1819 when Sir Stamford Raffles landed and secured it as a major trading post for Britain. Chinese workers were attracted to the tax-free outpost, and it remained in British control until 1942 when the Japanese invaded. The Brits were welcomed back after the war, but it was obvious Singapore would move towards independence.

RIGHT: The Merlion—a Singapore landmark
BELOW: A gold polisher in Little India

NEXT PAGE
LEFT ABOVE: Statue of Sir Stamford Raffles
LEFT BELOW: Tourist rickshaws in Little India, Singapore
RIGHT ABOVE: Manila's jeepneys in traffic
RIGHT BELOW: Singapore's Boat Quay

Although European, Malay and Indian culture remain an integral part of Singapore, its heart and soul is undoubtedly Chinese, and a visit to Chinatown is the best way to get acquainted with the dominant culture of Singapore. Street vendors hawk everything from fruit and vegetables to slabs of meat, fast food, Bhuddist symbols, lucky charms, shoe repairs, hair cuts, massages and fortune telling. It's also where the locals meet and eat, which is an essential part of Singaporean life, and a meal at one of Chinatown's busy food halls is an experience which is uplifting for the soul, and very easy on the wallet. In the chaotic clattering and confusion, ordering the food may seem a little tricky but a simple point-at-the-food-you-want strategy works perfectly well.

A bowl of noodles is the best way to prepare for another onslaught of shopping in this consumer paradise, but don't try and keep up with the locals. They keep going until well into the night, while laden with bags and boxes. If shopping was an Olympic sport, Singapore would be a nation of gold medal winners.

LITTLE INDIA

Singapore's reputation as a modern shopping paradise is well justified, and a great escape from the rampant consumerism is the tiny enclave known as Little India. As you emerge from the train station, it's like arriving in the centre of Mumbai and it's a vibrant and intoxicating slice of a culture that has not just survived, but thrived, in the heart of modern Asia. Little India has become one of Singapore's major attractions thanks to the fact that it's not only an authentic snapshot of the sub-continent, but it's also the island nation's finest example of a preserved historical district. From the main drag of Serangoon Road, which stretches for almost a kilometre, there is a complex network of smaller streets and alleyways. Here, the sari and gold shops provide an explosion of colour, the aromas of the spice shops and perfume shops compete, the smell of vat-cooked curries hang in the air, and the sounds of shrill Indian pop music blaring from shop fronts become a soundtrack.

Little India emerged in the 1850s, some 30 years after the foundation of modern Singapore by Sir Stamford Raffles. Indian migrants and former convicts who chose to remain had already become a regular feature of the area, and the first Hindu temples began to spring up during this period, the finest example of which is the Sri Veeramakaliamman temple on Serangoon Road, built in 1881. It only takes about half a day to explore the streets of this fascinating suburb, but no trip would be complete without experiencing an authentic curry at one of the hundreds of restaurants in the area. Locals say it's difficult to find a substandard meal because the competition is so fierce. One of the culinary specials of the area is the Fish Head Curry, which is exactly as it sounds, and is eaten with rice and vegetables. Eating the eyeballs is optional, although connoisseurs believe the tissue behind the eyeballs is the best part of the whole dish. The best piece of advice given by a regular Little India curry devotee is: follow your nose and if you see lots of Indians in the restaurant, then it must be good. But don't expect cutlery with your meal as the traditional way to eat is with your hands.

Thailand

It's a distinctly hot, busy and congested city and Bangkok is most visitors' first impression of Thailand. Despite its many physical flaws, it's hard not to leave with a sense of amusement and a desire to return. This is not the place where you'll find the fantastic beaches and beautiful waters seen in postcards and on travel shows—they're further south in the other cruise destinations of Phuket and Ko Samui—but what Bangkok does offer is a unique cityscape with the mighty Chao Phraya River running through its heart with an extensive system of khlongs, or canals, linking many of the suburbs to create a fascinating water world.

Despite its increasing modernisation, which is happening throughout Asia, there's still a strong sense of tradition in Bangkok with palaces, temples and shrines as the physical evidence of this. Despite the motorised madness, noise and smog, the people somehow retain a genuine cheery disposition. The port of Laem Chabang, an hour and a half south of Bangkok, is the closest cruise ships can get to the city, but the journey north is rewarded with one of the most endearing, and enduring, cities of Asia.

The Grand Palace on the banks of the Chao Phraya is the main tourist attraction in Thailand, and despite the crowds that routinely wander inside its walls, it's a grand introduction to Thai culture. Local people are among the hordes, and they go to worship and pray at the temples. On some days they outnumber the farang, or tourists. Set over nearly 220 sq km (136 sq miles), it's the former royal residence and is recognised as one of the most stunning architectural feats in Asia.

Sightseeing aside, shopping and eating are the main activities, and can be combined, with street markets surrounded by cheap noodle stalls and shopping malls stuffed with slightly more expensive versions of the same thing. The weekend market at Chatuchak doubles up as a sightseeing excursion, with its several thousand stalls selling almost every earthly possession from Thai silk and batik, to jewellery, 'designer' clothes which look like the real thing, handbags, dolls, precious stones, pottery, DVDs and music CDs at ridiculously cheap prices. In between the regular items, this is also the place of the bizarre with live snakes and weirdly cross-bred dogs for sale, deep fried insects for eating while an impromptu Country and Western band does a Kenny Rogers cover in Thai.

The phrase 'assault on the senses' is often used in relation to Bangkok and it's perhaps the best summary of a city that has to be seen and experienced to be believed.

BANGKOK'S KHLONGS

For centuries the people of Bangkok relied on its extensive system of rivers and canals for their existence, and although many networks have been reclaimed for development, there are still pockets in the city which are holding on to the past.

These canals, called *khlongs*, are the lifeblood of districts like Thon Buri and they provide the only means of transport in a water world far removed from the heat and traffic congestion of modern Bangkok. The local people live, eat, sleep, bathe and wash in the canals which serve as a natural road system. They're lined with houses ranging from quite smart multi-level homes to dilapidated wooden shacks, most decorated with Thai flags and posters of their revered King.

Since Bangkok was founded in 1782, the rivers and the natural and man-made canals made the city what it is today, with the mighty Chao Phraya River serving as the city's main artery. This is how Bangkok earned the nickname 'The Venice of the East', and in 1855 the British envoy Sir John Bowring wrote: 'The highways of Bangkok are not streets and roads, but the river and canals.' At this time three quarters of the 400,000 population lived in floating houses or on stilted homes on the canal banks. Today most of the canals have been filled in to make way for tarmac roads which service a growing population of 10 million, but there are enough *khlongs* remaining to provide a snapshot into Bangkok's historical past.

Instead of cars parked on the lawn, small canoes with a single paddle are tied up out front of the homes on stilts. The canoes are the main mode of transport for the locals, while the high-powered longtail boats are used for commuters who pay a small fee, or for *farang* (foreigners) to tour the area. Market traders also operate from these small canoes, offering a surprisingly vast array of goods ranging from fresh produce and bottled water for local shoppers, to colonial style hats and traditional Thai fans for tourists. Husband and wife teams also serve piping hot noodles from their mobile floating restaurants.

RIGHT: A river market trader
BELOW: Khlong kids

Vietnam

It's just after dawn on a hot and hazy morning and along the banks of the Saigon River, the families living in their fishing and market boats walk out onto deck to greet the new day. Daily life gets going early in this part of the world and since well before dawn, other junks and fishing boats have been putt-putting up and down the river in a ritual that's been going on every day of the week for centuries.

Fishing families brush their teeth and prepare breakfasts on the decks of their floating homes as our luxurious, state-of-the-art cruise liner cuts through the middle of the river, leaving a wake in its path. It's no wonder the locals briefly stop what they're doing and just stare.

Arriving into the heart of Ho Chi Minh City by ship offers a unique glimpse of the sublime Mekong Delta, and it's becoming a popular Asian detour for many cruise lines. The ports of Hong Gai, which serves the historic city of Hanoi, and Chan May for Hue and the ethereal islands of Halong Bay, are further to the north and are also being added to itineraries in the region.

If there's one stop only in Vietnam, then it's likely to be Ho Chi Minh City, because of the mesmerising Saigon River transit and the sudden, striking contrasts on land. From the moment you step onto the quay, you're transported from a sanitised, gleaming slice of Western life, into the frenetic-yet-friendly chaos that is Vietnam's largest city. You quickly learn several things. For one, Ho Chi Minh City is a mass of contradictions which can be as frustrating one moment as they are delightful the next. For another, it's also a city which cannot agree on its name: officials insist it's Ho Chi Minh City, but many of the local residents use its former name of Saigon.

But you also learn that sometimes the easiest of tasks can become the day's biggest challenge. Take crossing the road, for example. The second your feet touch the tarmac, bicycles and motorbikes of all types, and in all states of disrepair, bear down on you. The advice you're given is that you must not hesitate as the traffic will avoid you, but as a moped carrying a family of five and a truck laden with chickens whisk past on either side at breakneck speed, it's hard to be that confident.

What isn't hard to see, however, is that Ho Chi Minh City is a sprawling, dynamic and industrious centre—both the country's economic capital and its cultural trendsetter. It was modelled by the French in their own image, and much of their influence can still be seen today in its wide boulevards, architecture, and a devout Catholic population. Although there's little physical evidence of past wars on the surface, museums and monuments reveal this is a country that seems to have been in military conflict all its life with the exception of the past three decades.

Evidence of modernisation is apparent in some aspects of daily life in Ho Chi Minh City: from cafés where suited Vietnamese men hatch business deals on mobile phones, to urban teens posing in their fake designer street wear. Then there's the myriad of shops and stalls selling digital cameras, diving watches, TVs and DVD players. In Ho Chi Minh everyone is your friend and has something to sell, from the persistent-if-friendly cyclo drivers looking for a fare, to people selling kitsch souvenirs or volunteering their services as tour guides.

Although the jackhammers of progress are trying to pound the past into a pulp and throwing off the legacy of war, the tradition of this 300-year-old metropolis successfully retains its stranglehold on day-to-day life. The streets are where it all happens, amid the endless stalls and street markets with vendors selling everything from fake designer handbags to live fish and fruits from blankets spread across the uneven pavements. In the quiet pagodas monks pray and burn incense, while in the dusty alleys sandals are repaired by hand and children carefully roll out the rice paper that becomes spring rolls.

But that's Ho Chi Minh City in a nutshell—it's a city of colour and contrasts which churns, heaves, bubbles and fumes, and is a fascinating mix of east and west, past and future.

VIETNAMESE RICE PAPER—THE TRADITIONAL WAY

Vietnamese food is considered one of the healthiest cuisines in the world, as it's based primarily on raw vegetables and seafood, both of which are abundant in the country. Also, it does not involve a lot of deep frying. A popular Vietnamese dish is spring rolls, also known as summer rolls, and they differ from the Chinese variety in two ways. For one, they are made of wafer thin rice paper rather than a wheat-based dough; the paper is often so thin you can see the ingredients through it! But Vietnamese spring rolls also do not have to be deep fried. The traditional way of making Vietnamese rice paper, or bánh tráng, is passed through families, and taught even to the young children. On a trip there we were able to see how it's done by a young master.

First the rice is made into a thick paste by being broken down into a powder and mixed with water. To make the paper, a spoon of paste is dropped on a large, round steaming plate, and spread thinly using a spatula or spoon. Then the plate is covered with a lid to stop the steam from escaping, and the paper is steamed. Once it 'sets' (which only takes a couple of minutes) the sheet of paper is carefully removed from the plate and laid out to dry. A typical filling for Vietnamese spring rolls is rice noodles, shrimp, bean sprouts and carrots julienne style, and they are served with a dipping sauce such as spicy peanut. Today, however, tapioca starch is often being used in addition to, or as a substitute for, rice in the making of rice paper. There are a number of reasons for this, including that this type of paper doesn't require hot water for softening prior to use. But taste experts say that they lack the slight sourness that is the signature flavour of traditional rice paper.

Japan

With its mad mix of colossal neon, gleaming skyscrapers and ancient temples and shrines, today's Japan simultaneously embraces its rich history and latches onto the latest gadgets, gizmos and fashion trends. Its ancient culture may be thousands of years old and revered and respected by its inhabitants, but walk the city streets and you'll see modern cityscapes with men in suits and younger fashionistas with outrageous hairstyles and a dress style which may have been influenced by alien beings with a wicked sense of humour.

Some of the 'old' Japan remains in existence and occasionally a beautiful temple or serene garden can be found, but it will often be surrounded by a concrete jungle which provides a startling contrast. This mix of old and new is what really makes Japan interesting and Tokyo is often the first experience for newcomers to the country. The port of Yokohama services the city of 12 million people and this is the most popular destination in Japan, although Osaka and Kobe are interesting cities which also provide access to ancient Kyoto. The likes of Nagasaki and Shimonoseki are becoming more frequently visited.

LEFT: Akihabara, dubbed 'Electric Town' by day

NEXT PAGE
LEFT ABOVE: Akihabara
LEFT BELOW: Tokyo's Hibiya Park
RIGHT: Shiodome Shiosite at night

TOKYO

Japan's biggest city and capital continues to defy description and covering this vast metropolis is best done by subway which is a simple and efficient way of getting around. Japan, and Tokyo in particular, has a reputation as being a hyper-expensive destination but most of the major sights are actually free. From people-watching in Shinjuku to the so-called 'pleasure district' of Kabuki-cho with its crazy nightlife, restaurants, strip joints and love hotels, to the swanky designer fashion district of Ginza, Tokyo has a swag of suburbs each with their own unique personality.

In amongst the gaudy neon, crowds of people, and the din of the karaoke bars and pachinko parlours, elegant shrines and temples can be found including the Meiji Shrine and Asakusa Kannon, where the feeling of 'old Edo' prevails. Asakusa is also home of Nakamise Dori, the place to stock up on tacky souvenirs such as Japanese fans and doll key rings.

At some stage it makes sense to get a perspective of how this jigsaw puzzle of a city fits together and there are two places to take in panoramic views of the city, and only one comes with a price. The free option is from the 45th floor observatories at the Tokyo Metropolitan Government Buildings in Shinjuku. On a clear day, you can even see Mt Fuji. The view you pay for is atop the Mori Tower at Roppongi Hills. Occupying the 54th floor, Tokyo City View is a vast, glass-enclosed observation deck to which urban lovebirds and tourists flock an hour or so before sunset.

EATING OUT IN TOKYO ON THE CHEAP

A major misconception about eating out in Tokyo is that it costs a fortune. True, you can still blow a weekly wage at some five-star restaurants, but there are many affordable dining options; from local Japanese, to McDonald's, and a slew of Western-style cafes. With many Tokyoites leading hectic lifestyles, eating out for lunch has become almost as popular as eating out for dinner. As a result, many restaurants offer three-course set lunch deals for around 1,000 yen ($US10), and conveyor-belt sushi eateries can charge as little as 105 yen ($US1.00) per dish. Tokyo's department store food halls, called depachika, are another option, with everything from traditional bento box meals to salads, and western favourites. Other havens for inexpensive food such as ramen, yakitori and tempura include markets, temples and shrines. And if you're after Tokyo-style fast food, look out for chain restaurants called Yoshinoya and Matsuya. The food is basic but good quality and it's served at lightning speed.

KYOTO

Packed with impressive sights and natural beauty, Kyoto is one of the world's most culturally impressive cities. For those who have a romanticised image of Japan as an idealised feudal country of teahouses and temples, castles and bamboo forests, sliding rice paper screens and raked gravel gardens, their preconceived ideas may be jolted by the brashness of Tokyo. If Japan's capital city is a vision of the country's future, then Kyoto is a bridge to its past.

Kyoto, Japan's former imperial capital, is one of the few cities in Japan unscathed by World War II. It has been touched by modern life, but much of its early heritage remains; it has over 1600 Bhuddist temples, 200 Shinto shrines and three imperial palaces. It's also home to a fifth of Japan's national treasures and has no less than 17 World Heritage Sites, of which Kinkaku-ji is one.

Kinkaku-ji, the location of the Temple of the Golden Pavilion, is just one of the many atmospheric settings in Kyoto used for the film adaptation of Arthur Golden's bestseller *Memoirs of a Geisha*, along with Nijo Castle which was built in 1603 as the official residence of the first Tokugawa Shogun Ieyasu, in his day, one of the most powerful men in Japan. It's a sprawling collection of ancient architecture and gardens dominating central Kyoto. Each beautifully maintained building tells the story of an important era in Japan's history. And of great amusement to visitors today are the corridors with built-in 'nightingale' floors, created to warn the shogun of intruders. Even the lightest step makes the wooden floor sing like the bird it's named for.

The temple of Kiyomizu-dera is another of Kyoto's World Heritage Listed sites. Tucked into the low mountains on the eastern side of the city, it was first built in 798 and is devoted to Juichi-men Kannon, a Buddhist deity with 11 heads. The present buildings are reconstructions which date back to 1633, and perched high above the city they offer sweeping views of Kyoto and its surrounds. Filmgoers will recognise its soaring pagodas, which were also frequently used as cutaways in *Memoirs of a Geisha*.

PREVIOUS PAGE
LEFT ABOVE: View of Kyoto from Kiyomizu-dera
LEFT BELOW: Shinjuku at night
RIGHT: Kiyomizu-dera Pagoda, Kyoto

LEFT: Two maiko in Kyoto

Apart from sightseeing, which can be overwhelming in a place like Kyoto, geisha spotting is another favourite past-time and the district of Gion is the place to go for a sighting of the famous 'painted ladies'. Geisha are female artists who spend years training in the arts to entertain powerful men, typically in a teahouse called an ochaya. In Kyoto, they call themselves geiko, and the striking young women with white makeup, ornate black hair and bright kimonos who attract the most attention are apprentices, called *maiko*.

Gion is like a picture postcard of an almost-vanished Japan. It's a compact neighbourhood of narrow, stone-flagged streets lined with restored wooden buildings, dubbed 'the bedrooms of eels' by locals because of their long, narrow design. The pre-World War II era in which *Memoirs* was set is regarded as the end of the golden era for Kyoto's geisha community. From 3,000 in the early 19th century, today their numbers have dwindled to around 280, and most of them live and work here. Spotting a real one isn't easy as their numbers have declined and you're more likely to see an American tourist who has been 'made over', although with patience and good fortune it's possible.

CHEFS AT SEA, NOBU MATSUHISA

Known to the world simply as 'Nobu' an air of celebrity undoubtedly surrounds the highly acclaimed Japanese chef, Nobu Matsuhisa. A classically trained sushi-chef who dreamed of seeing the world, his culinary journey began when he opened his own sushi bar in Peru. From there he travelled the globe developing his unique 'Nobu style' of cuisine, an innovative blend of classically styled Japanese foods, with distinct Peruvian and European influences. In 1987, Nobu opened his first full-service restaurant, Matsuhisa in Beverly Hills, which became an overnight success. And in the 20 years which have followed, in addition to receiving a litany of awards, both Nobu's reputation and his empire of highly respected restaurants have expanded globally. The master chef is also behind two unique specialty restaurants at sea. Called Silk Road and The Sushi Bar, both feature on Crystal Cruises' two luxurious ships, the *Crystal Serenity* and the *Crystal Symphony*.

'For me cooking is most about giving my customers little surprises that will lead them to make discoveries about their own latent tastes. It's about communicating my kokoro, a Japanese term for heart, through every single dish I make. But there are special challenges reproducing my cuisine on a cruise ship. My signature dishes require the best ingredients and have to be fresh, but fortunately, new freezing and chilling technology ensures we can fulfill our high standards and customers' expectations. On a day-to-day basis, the food in Silk Road and The Sushi Bar is prepared by executive chefs who have experience in my land-based restaurants. I trained them myself, and I select my staff in the same way that I choose fish. Everything has to be the pick of the catch. One thing I do enjoy is the relationships between the guests in my restaurants at sea. It is what makes fine dining on a ship so special. You can have intimate contact with guests that is not possible in a big city where everyone's in a hurry.'

Cocktails

Red Lotus

1 part vodka
1 part lychee liqueur
1 part cranberry juice

Mix all ingredients in a cocktail shaker with ice, shake well,
strain into small martini glass, and serve.

Singapore Sling

2 parts gin
1 part cherry brandy
1 part fresh lemon juice
Dash of soda water
A strip of lemon rind

Add the gin, cherry brandy and lemon juice into a highball glass with ice,
top up with soda water, garnish with the lemon peel and serve.

RIGHT: Red Lotus

Recipes

Cold Hokkien Noodles with Smoked Cod & Prawns

300g (10oz) of cooked hokkien noodles, cold
4 king prawns, cooked
4 small fillets of smoked cod
8 broccolini florets
2 tbsp cod roe
2 cloves of garlic, crushed
1 tbsp of sesame oil

Stir fry the broccolini with the garlic in the sesame oil, and set aside to cool. In a separate pan, poach the fish fillets in a combination of coconut milk and water, and set aside to cool. Then take the cooked prawns, peel off the entire shell, and cut lengthwise so that the prawn can be laid flat.

To serve, divide the noodles into four servings, and layer the remaining ingredients, starting with a place a piece of fish, a prawn, one or two florets and top with a little of the cod roe.

Serves four

Fortune Cookies

4 large eggs
1 tsp vanilla extract
1 tsp almond extract
6 tbsp vegetable oil
250g (9oz) flour
3 tsp cornflour
½ tsp salt
250g (9oz) sugar
6 tsp water

Type or hand write 20 fortunes on small strips of paper. Separate the eggs, and in a mixing bowl, lightly beat the egg whites, vanilla and almond extracts, and the vegetable oil until frothy. In a separate bowl, sift the cornflour, salt and sugar, and stir in the water. Add the mixture to the egg white, and stir until you have a smooth batter.

Lightly grease four 22 x 33cm (9 x 13in) baking sheets. Place level tablespoons of the batter onto the sheet at least 7–8cm (3in) apart. Gently tilt the sheet back and forth and from side to side, so that each spoon of batter forms a circle. Bake in the oven at 150°C (300°F) until the cookies are golden brown. Remove each cookie quickly with a spatula, turn over, and place a fortune in the centre. To make the cookie shape, fold the cookie in half and gently pull the edges downwards over the rim of a thin bowl.

Makes 20 cookies

Black Cod in Miso
(Supplied by Chef Nobu Matsuhisa)

4 black cod fillets, about 220g (½lb) each
4 stalks hajikami ginger pickled in sweet vinegar

Nobu–style Saikyo Miso
Sake
¾ cup mirin
2 cups white miso paste
225g (8oz) granulated sugar

First, bring the sake and mirin to the boil in a medium saucepan over a high heat. Boil for 20 seconds to evaporate the alcohol. Turn the heat down and add the miso paste, mixing with a wooden spoon. When the miso has dissolved completely, turn the heat up to high again and add the sugar, stirring constantly to ensure that the bottom of the pan doesn't burn. Remove from heat once the sugar is fully dissolved, and cool to room temperature.

Pat the fish fillets dry with paper towels. Slather the fish with Nobu-style Saikyo Miso and place in a nonreactive dish or bowl and cover tightly with plastic wrap. Leave to steep in the refrigerator for two or three days.

When ready to cook, preheat a grill or the broiler setting of your oven. Lightly wipe off any excess miso clinging to the fish fillets but don't rinse it off. Place the fish on the grill, or in a broiler pan, and grill or broil until the surface of the fish turns brown. Then bake at 205°C (400°F) for 10 to 15 minutes.

To serve, take the ginger and briefly plunge into a pot of boiling water. Then arrange the black cod fillets on individual plates and garnish with the hajikami. Add a few drops of Nobu-style Saikyo Miso to each plate.

Serves four

White Fish Tiradito Nobu Style

500g (18oz) red snapper fillet
Rocoto chili paste
coriander leaves, stems removed
1 tbsp plus 1 tsp yuzu juice (Japanese citrus juice)
2 tbsp plus 2 tsp lemon juice
sea salt

Cut the fish into paper-thin slices and arrange on a plate. Put a coriander
leaf and a small dollop of rocoto chili paste on each slice, and then drizzle
the yuzu and lemon juice over all pieces. To serve, sprinkle with sea salt to
taste, bearing in mind that the flavor of this dish depends on the salt—if
too little is used it will taste bland.

Serves four

South Pacific South

05:
South Pacific

The islands of the South Pacific conjure up images of vast mountains rising straight up out of the ocean, stunning white sand beaches, palm trees swaying in the breeze and sunsets that light the sky in a wild palette of outrageous colours. It's a region that lives up to its tropical clichés and the island groups and their inhabitants are inextricably bound by a common culture which is as fascinating as it is enduring.

A seafaring race, the Polynesian people may have spread throughout the islands over thousands of years, and over many thousands of miles, but they remain unified in their deep respect for their ancient principles, their physical environment, and for their family and local communities. They're proud of their heritage, which has been passed down through the generations in the form of storytelling, and the genuine warmth of the people of the South Pacific is an important part of its appeal. Whether you're in Tahiti, Hawaii or Fiji, it is possible to find that slice of paradise on some of the most spectacular islands in the world.

LEFT: A private atoll, Motu Mahana
BELOW: The *Paul Gauguin* at Hanaveve Bay, Fatu Hiva

Tahiti & Her Islands

It's a region that's inspired generations of artists and writers, and cruising French Polynesia's islands it's easy to see why. Perfect blue lagoons, colourful reefs, volcanic mountains, bright flowers and a real atmosphere of tranquility combine to create one big natural water-colour that typifies the tropical idyll. French Polynesia, more popularly known as Tahiti and Her Islands, is divided into five separate archipelagos—the Society Islands which includes the main island of Tahiti and the administrative capital of Papeete, the Marquesas, the Tuamotus, and the remote and tiny Australs and Gambier Archipelago. Each group is unique and was formed by volcanic activity, creating mountainous islands and coral atolls, or reefs which are just above the water surface, surrounded by a natural lagoon.

Famous for its overwater bungalows and five-star resorts, there's a lot more to Tahiti than sipping cocktails under a palm tree by a pool (although there's absolutely nothing wrong with that). With 118 islands spread out over an area just a little smaller than Europe, Tahiti and Her Islands is best experienced from the water as this is truly one of the world's great maritime destinations. Many of the more remote islands can only be reached by ship, and this is where the 'real' Tahiti exists with a genuine reverence among the people for their cultural heritage.

THE SOCIETY ISLANDS

It's just after 6pm and time for the nightly sunset show as the first tinge of yellow permeates the horizon. With the mythical peaks of Bora Bora as the backdrop, the show quickly moves into full swing. From yellow to orange, pink, red, blue, purple—and various outrageous hues in between—the multi-coloured palette moves through the sky and glassy ocean. With the sky ablaze, outrigger canoes paddle through the surreal scene and out in the middle of one of the lagoons that ring the island, the jagged volcanic mountains on each side change colour with the sunset and finally darken against the night sky.

The name Bora Bora has become synonymous with the word 'paradise', and with its emerald-green hills and chameleon-like lagoons, it's easy to understand why it's a serious contender for the most beautiful and romantic island in the world. James Michener, author of *Tales of the South Pacific* which inspired the movie *Bali Hai*, wrote of Bora Bora: 'Anyone who has ever been there wants to go back.' Sailing into Bora Bora means navigating the one and only entry point through the reef surrounding the island, the Teavanui Pass, and is one of those experiences which burns unforgettable images and emotions into the memory. Like many of the Tahitian islands, Bora Bora was created out of a volcano and the jagged peaks which rise out of the ocean mark the edge of the original crater. Although it's around 260km (160 miles) northwest of the main island of Tahiti, it's often the first stop for cruises in this region because of the 'wow' factor that comes with circling Bora Bora before making the grand entrance into the lagoon.

But 'the magical island' of Moorea is no less alluring. It's also been credited for inspiring the mythical *Bali Hai*, and appropriately, it's a heart-shaped island with a dramatic landscape which mirrors Bora Bora. Also a volcanic island, Moorea is a heady mix of mountains which often reach the clouds, tropical jungles, beautiful lagoons and the ocean, which form a landscape of deep blue and green. Unlike Bora Bora however, there are several passes which allow ships to navigate past the reef which surrounds Moorea and sail into the turquoise lagoons. The *Passe Teavaroa* and *Passe Tareu* on the northern side of the island are the most used passes by cruise ships and allow entry into Cook's Bay and Opunohu Bay. Cook's Bay is the most developed area of the island with a string of hotels on the water alongside the main village of Paopao, but Opunohu Bay is arguably the most beautiful place on the island and is much quieter. It's been the setting for many films including the the third remake of *Mutiny on the Bounty* starring Anthony Hopkins and a young Mel Gibson. Quite simply, Opunohu Bay, and much of Moorea, possesses a powerful and natural beauty which even attracts Tahitians from other islands, and especially from the main island of Tahiti as it's only a 20km (12 mile) ferry ride across the Sea of the Moon.

That's not to say the other Society Islands are unworthy of attention. The twin islands of Ra'iatea and Taha'a, which are separated by a three kilometre channel and share a coral reef and a protected lagoon, are less touristy than Bora Bora and Moorea but have a more traditional Polynesian feel with a laid-back atmosphere. Ra'iatea is known as 'the Sacred Island' as it was the centre of Tahitian royalty, religion, and culture, and today its main attraction is the massive Taputapuata *marae*, the largest and most sacred site in Polynesia. It's also one of several places to check out one of Tahiti's most prized souvenirs and famous exports; black pearls. Taha'a is the smaller of the twin islands and even quieter than Ra'iatea, but 'the Vanilla Island' possesses a genuine village atmosphere, perhaps due in part to the fact that there's very little traffic. It's main claim to fame, however is vanilla production and a string of beautiful *motu*, uninhabited coral islets with stunning beaches, on its northern side.

As for the main island, most visitors bypass Tahiti and its capital Papeete and simply connect to the outer islands, and miss out on its charms. From the street life of Papeete, to a four-wheel drive tour of the interior with its cascading waterfalls and ancient *marae*, or archaeological sites, or simply catching some sun and snorkelling off the beaches at Punaauia, the main island possesses its own unique attractions. The municipal market in Papeete, *Le Marché*, features every conceivable fruit and vegetable from the islands on the ground floor while the second floor is dedicated to Tahitian arts and crafts. If given a chance the main island can reveal a cultural side of its people and history that the glitzy resort islands don't offer. What it lacks in the classic-island-postcard stakes it makes up for with a very authentic French colonial charm.

MOTU MAHANA

One of the highlights of nearly every m/s *Paul Gauguin* cruise in Tahiti is a day spent on Motu Mahana. It's a private island for Regent Cruises guests only and this idyllic motu is flanked by Taha'a's mountains on one side and Bora Bora's cloud-piercing peaks on the other. Shimmering lagoon water laps gently against the edges of a pristine white beach dotted with teak deck chairs, umbrellas and hammocks strung between palm trees. The flowers are incredible, as colourful sprays of bougainvillea spill over the trees and pathways, and tropical hibiscus with their pink and scarlet petals face up at the sun. The unavoidable lure of the warm, crystal clear waters can turn even the most sedentary beach lover into a snorkeller or kayaker, and thanks to a floating bar, it's also possible to wallow in the balmy water sipping a Pina Colada made in a fresh coconut, while colourful fish dart about your feet.

The day on Motu Mahana is also the perfect opportunity to sample traditional Tahitian cuisine in a tropical paradise setting, from starters like poisson cru (tuna marinated in coconut milk and lime), to grilled local fish like mahi mahi, roast suckling pig, with side servings of yam and taro. Although the main ingredients are fairly basic, French and Chinese influences means they can all be prepared in different styles, from fish or meat cooked in either coconut milk, garlic or curry to simple grills with tropical fruit on the side, Tahitian cuisine has taken on an international flavour which is heavily influenced by the fresh produce unique to the region.

LEFT: The *Paul Gaugun* in Hiva Oa, Tahiti

LEFT BELOW: Local dancers from Omoa Village, Fatu Hiva

RIGHT: Hibiscus at Hiva Oa

THE MARQUESAS

As the m/s *Paul Gauguin* cruises into Omoa Bay, the eerie sounds of conch shells and drums pounding out a driving rhythm increase in intensity. Volcanic cliffs almost one kilometre high drop straight into the ocean, and in between are deep gorges with lush jungle. It's a surreal arrival into one of the most remote and unspoiled of the Tahitian Isles, Fatu Hiva. There are no airports, no jetties, no marinas and a concrete slab at the end of the point on Omoa Bay is the only way on and off the island via an inflatable zodiac. On many days, big swells make it impossible to set foot on Fatu Hiva, and this fact in itself sums up the essence of the Marquesas.

They don't get many visitors, but when they do a buzz goes around the 500 or so inhabitants who turn out in traditional dress to greet the new arrivals, beating drums and singing traditional songs. In the main square, local artisans set up and display their handmade creations and it's easy to see why Marquesan handicrafts are regarded as among the most authentic and beautiful cultural creations in Polynesia. A traditional dance is performed but this is not a 'show' as performed by professional troupes in five-star resorts in the Society Islands. It's a show of village pride and an authentic snapshot into Marquesan culture.

Located nearly one and a half thousand kilometres north-east of the main island of Tahiti, the Marquesas' isolation means they are relatively untouched by tourism. A smile from a local is genuine, and when they want to take you around their village they don't expect to get paid, they're just showing off their lifestyle and heritage. Of the twelve islands that make up the group, just six are inhabited (only four with tiny air strips) and flights are infrequent and expensive.

Around Omoa Village, and in nearby Hanaveve Village, fruits grow wild by the roadside and in between the houses are coconuts, breadfruit, local mountain apples, oranges, mangoes, papayas, bananas, avocados and Tahitian grapefruit (pampelmousse) which is twice as large as a normal grapefruit and so much sweeter than most varieties. The breadfruit grows on trees up to 20 metres (65ft) tall and is an important starch of Marquesas which can be roasted, boiled or baked. The fishing boats bobbing next to the quai are evidence that seafood is also one of the staple foods for the locals, as are the children using bamboo poles and hand lines to catch fish, while further inland families cast nets to catch freshwater shrimp from rivers at the back of the valley.

The Marquesas possess a powerful and overwhelming physical presence and sheer volcanic cliffs rise dramatically out of the Pacific Ocean. The jagged peaks rise side-by-side more than a kilometre up, creating plateaus at high altitude and steep valleys with lush vegetation which are home to wild horses and goats brought by European settlers. Most of the Marquesan Islands feature partly sunken caldera, which create a natural amphitheatre among the towering mountains and this is where the villagers choose to settle. The locals call their region *Te Henua Enana* which means 'the Land of Men' in reverence to their stunning backdrop.

The history of Tahiti and Her Islands can also be traced back to the Marquesas. The first Polynesians arrived in 300AD as part of a migration from South East Asia, which was around five hundred years before settlement in the Society Islands. Only a very jaded traveller wouldn't fall for French Polynesia's beauty and charm; the dramatic landscapes, the exotic flowers, the crystal clear waters, and the sunsets which light up the sky and ocean in a 360-degree panorama of magnificent colours.

GAUGUIN'S TAHITI

Many people have fallen for the extraordinary charms of Tahiti and Her Islands, and among the most famous is the legendary French artist, Paul Gauguin. He arrived in Tahiti in 1891 financially ruined, in search of a new life, and determined to discover as much as he could about the Polynesian peoples and their culture. But the exotic idyll he'd imagined wasn't what he saw when he stepped off the steamer docked in Papeete. The Pacific island was a colony, with French officials and soldiers strutting around much the same as they did back home, the two things from which he was trying to escape. In the years which followed, however, Gauguin painted what he saw or imagined the real Tahiti to be: well-rounded women wearing colourful pareu (sarongs), long haired warriors riding bareback along the beaches, and locals washing horses in the foaming surf.

Although Gauguin lived on Tahiti for much of the 1890s, he spent his last years on the Marquesas Island of Hiva Oa, one of the northernmost islands of French Polynesia, and died of syphillis in 1903. He is buried in Calvaire Cemetary, which is perched on top of a hill above Hiva Oa's main town of Atuona, overlooking the romantically named Bay of Traitors. Gauguin's grave is made of red sandstone and shaded by a frangipani tree, with one of Tahiti's legendary landscapes as a backdrop—jagged mountains draped in lush, green tropical foliage. His descendants are said to be scattered all over French Polynesia and some are said to have distinctly European features, while others are rumoured to bear his trademark red hair. But for any visitor to the Marquesas, a walk around the island is evidence enough that the Tahiti Gauguin depicted in such vivid colour and form lives on.

Hawai'i

The name evokes images of beaches lined with palm trees teased by an ocean breeze, white sand beaches, stunning mountains, tropical forests, waterfalls, bikinis and cocktails, and Hawai'i is the epitome of carefree summer fun in the tropics. When Elvis Presley hit the silver screen in 1961 in *Blue Hawaii*, the legend of this carefree South Seas paradise was confirmed around the world as the place to go for singing, dancing and romancing in a beautiful setting. The Hawaiian island chain, like French Polynesia, is volcanic and made up of hundreds of islands spread out over 2,400 kilometres, with eight 'main islands' in the archipelago—O'ahu, Maui, Kaua'i, Hawai'i (also known as the Big Island), and the more remote islands of Ni'ihau, Moloka'i, Lana'i and Kaho'olawe. Each of the islands offers something unique to travellers who often argue over which of them is 'the best' and cruising the archipelago is a great way to settle the debate.

O'AHU

As the sun shifts slowly downwards towards the horizon, it deepens in colour to a fiery red, casting a wild fusion of colours across the ocean and onto one of the world's most famous beaches. Waikiki's charisma and unabashed sense of fun is on full display and as the water changes colour with the sunset. Surfers, body boarders, swimmers, outrigger canoes, kayakers and yachties all compete for space in the bay, and rising up behind all this is the famous city skyline and Diamond Head, the extinct volcanic crater that towers over the southern end of O'ahu. The truth is that O'ahu is often overlooked in the which-island-is-best debate, perhaps because of the tourist suburb of Waikiki on the South Shore. It's the island's major attraction and in recent years it's shrugged off its reputation as a tacky tourist trap thanks to a multi-million dollar 'facelift'.

The trash is gone, the streets have been widened and made more pedestrian-friendly, and the transformation has been embraced by hotels, restaurants and bars which have also been spruced up. In the past Waikiki evoked images of congested streets and weary hotels inhabited by loud 'mainlanders' in Hawaiian shirts sucking on cheap cigars, but now a more sophisticated crowd is heading to the island of O'ahu. Despite the gentrification, Waikiki is still an exciting place and its original appeal remains: hordes of holidaymakers sunbathe on the white sand, and out in the warm water hundreds of board-riders indulge themselves in one of the most famous and forgiving surf breaks in the world.

Waikiki has an allure which pulls in six million visitors a year, and many of those never leave its four square kilometre area on the southern end of O'ahu. But the rest of the island has a physical diversity which is well worth exploring. The eastern, or windward, side of O'ahu has some spectacular coastline without the crowds, and beaches such as Haunama Bay are protected by coral reef from the surf and are fantastic for snorkelling and swimming. The magnificent Ko'olau cliffs rise 900m (3,000ft) on the east coast and the Nu'uanu Pali Lookout doesn't just offer views of the magnificent formation, it's also a major historical site. In 1795 Kamehameha I fought and won a major battle by forcing his enemies over the
cliff. A little further along the east coast and tucked in under the Ko'olau cliffs near Kane'ohe is one of the most serene places on O'ahu, the Valley of the Temples. Built in 1968, it's a unique cemetery for both Christians and Bhuddists set on sprawling and peaceful hills. One building in particular stands out and the Byodo-In Temple is an exact replica of a temple in Uji, Japan, built over 900 years ago. Its beautiful architecture, koi ponds, peaceful gardens and the fantastic mountain backdrop make this a place of surreal calm.

The sleepy North Shore also provides a good antidote to the craziness of Waikiki and its 12km (7.5 mile) stretch of white sand fringed by palm trees is also the location of one of the world's best, and most famous, surf breaks. Waimea Bay is the centre of North Shore, and it sits alongside the Mecca of surfing in Banzai Pipeline and for those good enough to take on its seemingly impossible waves, a lifetime of bragging rights is the reward. Sunset Beach is also steeped in surfing folklore and, as the name suggests, this is the place to be at the end of a day. But if you happen to return to Waikiki, the sunsets are no less spectacular.

HISTORY OF SURFING

In 1778, on Captain Cook's third expedition to the Pacific, HMS *Discovery* and Resolution made the first recorded European visits to Hawai'i, stopping at the Big Island of Hawai'i. In Cook's journals, completed after his death by Lieutenant James King, two full pages were devoted to an in-depth description of surfboard riding, as practised by the locals on the Kona coast. But surfing, either lying down or standing up on long, hardwood boards, was nothing new in these islands. Although surfing's exact origins are the subject of debate, by the time the Europeans arrived the sport was deeply rooted in many centuries of Hawaiian legend and culture and was an integral part of daily life, layered into society, religion and myth. But Cook's visit left a wake which was to change Hawai'i forever, and throw both Hawaiian culture, and the ritual significance of surfing, into a sharp decline.

In the early 1900s, however, the antics of a young Hawaiian athlete from Waikiki called Duke Paoa Kahanamoku was set to be the catalyst which would transform surfing from a lost art into one of the world's most popular pastimes. Duke was already a famous swimmer, having won gold medals at the Olympic Games in 1912 and 1916, but he was also an avid surfer, and the surfing demonstrations he gave in California and Australia on hand-carved, hardwood longboards caused something of a sensation. The world sat up, took notice, and surfing was back on the map. Duke, who's dubbed 'the father of modern surfing' died in 1968, but today two monuments stand on opposite sides of the Pacific Ocean in his honour. One is opposite Freshwater Beach in Manly, New South Wales. But the other, and the more recognised of the two, takes pride of place on Duke's local beach of Waikiki in Honolulu, welcoming visitors to Hawai'i with open arms.

MAUI

There's no doubting Maui is a surfing haven—from the benign beginners' breaks at the Lahaina Rockwall to classic big wave locations like Jaws, but there's more to this island than its endless aquatic pleasures. Sure you can surf, snorkel, scuba dive, swim, windsurf, parasail, go deep sea fishing, hike and horse ride much of its 180km (110 mile) coastline and 50km (30 miles) of beautiful beaches, but towering regally over the island is one of the Pacific's most stunning natural wonders.

Haleakala is the world's largest dormant volcano at 3,000 metres (1,000ft) with a massive crater that stretches twelve by four kilometres. Visitors to Haleakala National Park are warned to rug up for the ascent to the volcano, but many refuse to believe there are parts of the Hawaiian Islands that can drop below freezing. Forget sarongs and frangipanis, this place is all about skivvies and fog, and it's just one of the islands' many surprises. The summit of this active volcano (it last erupted around 1790) possesses an other-world atmosphere with deeply sculpted mountain ridges carpeted in rich colour which literally changes hue in the varying light. From brown to orange to red, the cinder desert landscape puts on an evocative show, and it's a stunning contrast to the tropical postcard-version of Hawaii which can be seen from the summit.

From here you can see why Maui is regularly voted 'The Best Island in the World' by glossy travel magazines. Tom Selleck (*Magnum PI*) has a large home on the road up to Haleakala and other celebrities who've reportedly bought into the island paradise include Pearl Jam lead singer Eddie Vedder, actor Woody Harrelson, and rumours constantly abound that film and music stars are on the lookout for a multimillion dollar slice of heaven on Maui. Its popularity has resulted in an increased urbanisation on the island, and traffic can become congested. Strip malls are going up at a rapid rate, but with more than 80 beaches it's possible to escape the reminders of modern life.

THE 'BIG' ISLAND

Perhaps the most diverse of the islands in the archipelago, with deserts, rainforests, black sand beaches, volcanoes and even snow-capped mountains, the Big Island is one of those places which seduces nature lovers with its vast array of outdoor activities. It's famous for having eleven different climate zones and while it lacks in the picture postcard clichés of white sand beaches and palm trees, it more than makes up for it as one of the South Pacific's true adventure playgrounds. It takes little time to work out that the first thing to do is go to Volcanoes National Park. Two of its five volcanoes are still active, one of which is the Kilauea Caldera, the longest continuously erupting volcano in the world. Here, it's possible to walk through lava tubes and over old lava flows, or hike along Devastation Trail with its bizarre moon-like landscape.

Throwing snowballs is not an activity normally associated with this part of the world, but it's possible to play in the snow on Mauna Kea in the winter months, or view the stars from its observatories, while hikers can also trek through the sacred Waipio Valley with its 700 metre cliffs and waterfalls. Most cruises at to the itinerary, an evening on the Big Island to sail past Kilauea, where molten lava spews forth from cracks in the rock and flows into the ocean, creating plumes of steam as it hits the water. Kilauea is the world's most active volcano and has been continually erupting since 1983 and it reportedly produces enough lava every day to resurface a 30km (19 mile) two-lane road.

LEFT: Kaua'i's famous Na Pali coastline
BELOW: Wailua Falls, Kauai

KAUA'I

The northernmost Hawaiian island, Kaua`i, is believed to be the first which Captain James Cook stumbled upon while sailing from Tahiti to North America in 1778. Its lush vegetation, waterfalls, barren desert, volcanic cliffs and classic beaches have earned it the reputation as the most beautiful and natural of all the Hawaiian islands. Most cruise ships arrive at the North Shore of Kaua`i for one very simple reason—the Na Pali Coast. With its fluted sea cliffs, Na Pali towers almost 1,000 metres (3,000ft) straight up from the lush, green valleys and white sand beaches below. It's a 35km (22 mile) stretch of imposing coastline which is difficult to reach by land (it's at least a two-day hike and local guides are essential), and this is one of those special places which are best viewed from the deck of a ship.

The gaping gulch of Waimea Canyon is just as imposing no land. Dubbed the 'Grand Canyon' of the Pacific, it's just over a kilometre-and-a-half wide (1 mile) and 19km (12 miles) long, its seemingly never-ending cliffs, gorges and valleys changing colour every few minutes. Although smaller than the Grand Canyon, it's arguably more beautiful and the scenic lookouts along the way make it difficult to travel the 60km (37 mile) Waimea Canyon Road in less than half a day. It's a world away from Elvis' Hawai'i of the early 1960s and a stunning and obvious reminder of the diversity of landscapes that make these islands more than just a clichèd Hollywood version of a South Seas paradise.

Fiji

With more than 300 islands, Fiji is the type of place which could take an entire life time to explore properly. Like other island nations, it's possible to hunker down in a resort on a nice beach under a palm tree, but out in the deep blue are destinations and cultures which will ignite the imagination and create a strong life-long impression. Cruising Fiji provides a unique way to experience the physical beauty of the islands, and uncover the true heart and soul of its people who have earned the reputation as being among the most genuinely friendly in the world. This is where remote beaches can be found with no footprints in the sand, and where the local people greet visitors with the all-encompassing welcome of 'bula' before introducing you to their families.

Fiji has an interesting blend of various cultures, namely Melanesian, Polynesian, Indian, European, and Chinese, and it's a mix which is reflected in Fijian food, language and architecture. The political and geographical hub of the country is Viti Levu, the country's largest island, and it's the point of arrival for most visitors. Although it's worthy of a couple of days of exploration, in truth it lacks the sheer beauty, classic beaches, and traditional culture of some of the outer islands. But the Fiji idyll which draws millions of visitors a year is found among the smaller islands which are slices of paradise dominated by white sand beaches, tropical forests, waterfalls, coral reefs, and an abundance of tropical fish, making it both a sun lover's, diver's and snorkeller's paradise.

THE MAMANUCA & YASAWA ISLANDS

These are Fiji's two main island groups. The closest to the mainland are the Mamanucas, a group of about 20 small islands just off the western coast of Viti Levu, in a lagoon formed between the Great Sea Reef and the mainland. Due to their proximity to Viti Levu, these islands, and especially Plantation, Castaway, and Treasure, are highly popular with day trippers. And among this group are some islands boasting elegant and exclusive five-star resorts, such as the islands of Malolo and Navini. But visitors in the know who are in search of the real heart and soul of Fiji travel to the more remote islands of the Yasawa Group, a mini-archipelago where the tropical idyll, and the essence of Fijian history and culture, are both a fact and way of life.

A typical day in this part of Fiji goes something like this: you're sitting in the crystal clear water, surrounded by stunning volcanic outcrops which rise straight up out of the ocean and further down the beach one of the friendly local dogs approaches with its tail wagging, waiting for an invitation. As the dog cools off next to you, a group of school children also appear on the beach, on their way home, and they wave and stand on the water's edge, jostling each other to ask the question: 'Where are you from?' It's a common conversation starter for the younger Fijians who are genuinely keen to find out about visitors to their islands. After an introduction to each and every child, the kids wander off up the beach and the dog, called Draki, runs after them.

The Yasawas is a group of 17 volcanic islands which stretch over 90 kilometres, and are located off the north-western coast of Viti Levu, and they have a combined population of just 5,000. Of these remote islands a stand-out is Sawa I Lau. Located just off the larger Yasawa Island, most visiting cruise ships moor in the narrow bay between the two islands to create the impression that a new film set has been built with a panoramic vista of the towering peaks, perfect beaches and bays, and impossibly-blue water. Further north is Fiji's second largest island Vanua Levu with its near-neighbour Taveuni, known as the Garden Isle, and these islands are separated by the narrow Somosomo Strait and provide a different experience altogether. Vanua Levu, with its black sand beaches and gritty working towns, has some excellent diving, while Taveuni is a hikers' dream with lush forests and waterfalls and some stunning lookouts. Seen from the ocean, both islands impose themselves against the skyline and each year more and more cruise lines are discovering their unique qualities.

It's hard not to be drawn in by Fiji's colourful visual arts. Despite modern European influences, traditional village life on Fiji's outer islands remains true to its past and indigenous society is highly communal. Each village has a chief as the community leader and great emphasis is placed on the importance of family and traditional culture. The *meke*, or dance performance which tells a history of the village, is one of the principal ways indigenous Fijians maintain their links with the past. Each village has its own individual *meke* which is performed in the local dialect, many of which have been handed down through many generations. It's literally a history which has been preserved in oral form, and elders in a village ensure the link is never broken by passing on the ritual to the children. It doesn't take long to slip into 'Fiji time' and on the outer islands it's easy to slow down to local pace and start looking at life in the same way: no hurry, no rush, no problem. It's an infectious attitude from a people which have proudly hung onto their heritage, and a love of life itself.

Another unique Fijian experience which lives on in the Yasawas is the *meke wesi*, or men's spear dance, a narrative of a past war which is usually victorious. A typical performance goes like this: as the pace of the music and chanting intensifies, so too does the threatening gestures of the men holding spears as they stride towards the watching crowd in a menacing manner. Several of the 'warriors' have entered a trance-like state and throw their heads back, whirling madly in circles and continue the dance until the music suddenly stops. Everyone is quiet for a few seconds, and then the local children burst into a raucous laughter, and the adults and the dancers themselves follow suit. Although the meki wesi is taken very seriously when it's being performed in Fiji, it obviously provides light relief to everyone in the village when finished. After all these 'ferocious warriors' are actually fun loving dads, uncles or brothers to most of the spectators.

THE YAQONA CEREMONY

Another of indigenous Fiji's traditions is the *Yaqona* ceremony, or village welcome, which is taken very seriously as the pillar of social etiquette, and in some places it's a semi-religious experience. Before entering a village it's considered polite to seek permission, which usually results in meeting the local chief, and it's good manners to arrive with a *sevusevu*, or gift, of kava. As with all traditional villages, visitors should dress appropriately for the occasion which means covering shoulders and knees, and no hats. The local men prepare for the ceremony by pounding kava roots into a fine dust. Water is added to the kava and strained through cloth which produces the famous brown drink. The *Yaqona* Ceremony often takes place inside the community hall and local villagers are usually dressed in their traditional clothing. Visitors remove shoes outside the hall, with men standing in the front and women at the back (it's not sexist, it's a patriarchal society) and as a group the men call out 'dua, dua, dua' which informs the villagers they're ready to enter. They respond with 'O dua, dua, dua' which gives permission to enter.

If you're with a group, one of you kneels and presents the village with the kava and asks permission to visit their village and for their protection. It's polite to say that it's an honour to experience the culture and hospitality of the village. A village representative then accepts the *sevusevu* (gift of the kava) and gives permission to meet with the people and use their beaches. The actual kava drinking ceremony then begins in complete silence. The elder of the village presents the visiting representative with the first bowl. You clap once before receiving the bowl and say 'bula', which literally means 'life', and then drink the kava in one go. All the men then clap three times as a sign of respect. After that the kava bowl is passed to each of the main dignitaries. After about 15 minutes, the ceremony is completed and everyone in the hall is invited one-by-one to have a bowl of kava. This is when the formalities end and the atmosphere becomes a lot more relaxed.

Cocktails

Mai Tai

1 part dark rum
1 part white rum
1 part Cointreau
1 part lime juice
a dash of orange syrup
2 maraschino cherries and a wedge of pineapple to garnish

Fill a tall glass with crushed ice, and build ingredients in order.
Garnish with the pineapple and cherries, and serve.

Blue Pacific

2 parts gin
1 part Blue Curacao
1 dash of orange bitters
castor sugar
an orange wheel to garnish

Half fill a cocktail shaker with crushed ice, add liquid ingredients and shake
well. Rim a champagne saucer with the castor sugar, strain ingredients into
glass, garnish with the orange wheel and serve.

LEFT: Mai Tai

Recipes

Swordfish with Salad Niçoise

6 fillets of swordfish
6 eggs
10 Kipfler or new potatoes
3 egg or Roma tomatoes, cored and cut into lengths
1 small red onion thinly sliced
225g (8oz) French beans
¼ cup sliced black olives
1 tbsp capers
12 anchovy fillets
salt
freshly ground black pepper

Vinaigrette
½ cup lemon juice
¾ cup extra-virgin olive oil
1 medium shallot, minced
1 tsp fresh oregano, minced
1 tsp dijon mustard
salt and freshly ground black pepper

Place all the ingredients for the vinaigrette in a bowl, whisk, and set aside. Then hard boil the eggs, cool in water, peel, and cut into quarters. In another pan of water, cook the potatoes until tender and cut into halves. Put the tomatoes, beans, olives, capers and anchovy fillets, and the vinaigrette in a bowl and toss well. Then add the potatoes and toss one more time. Pan fry or grill the sword fish until cooked. To serve, divide the salad equally between six plates, top the salad with a piece of swordfish, and garnish with four pieces of egg.

Serves six

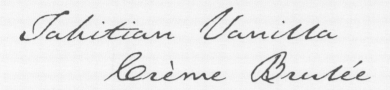

Tahitian Vanilla Crème Brûlée

2 cups whipping cream
1 cup of sugar
1 Tahitian vanilla bean cut lengthwise
½ tsp of vanilla extract
8 egg yolks
1 whole egg
140g (5oz) sugar

Place six ramekins in a large baking pan. In a saucepan, mix together the cream and sugar, then scrape the vanilla seeds into mixture and drop in the pods. On a low-to-medium heat, stir the mixture constantly and bring to a very gentle simmer. Cover and reduce heat for about 10 minutes. Whisk the egg yolks in a bowl, then add the hot cream mixture until it is just blended, and divide evenly among ramekins.

Pour enough hot water into the baking pan to measure about halfway up the sides of the ramekins, then bake the custards at 160°C (325°F) for about half an hour, or until they are almost set in the middle. Carefully remove the ramekins from the oven, allow them to cool. Sprinkle the top of each custard with around 1–2 teaspoons sugar, and place under a hot grill until sugar melts and browns. Allow to cool, then refrigerate for 2–4 hours. To serve, garnish with fruit.

Serves six

Tahitian Style Marinated Tuna (Poisson Cru)

1 kg (2.2 lb) sashimi grade tuna
300g (10½oz) fresh tomatoes
300g (10½oz) carrots
300g (10½oz) cucumber
200g (7oz) white onion, finely sliced
4 tsp fresh ginger, minced
2 cups white vinegar
100ml (3½fl oz) lime juice
2 cups coconut milk (fresh if possible)
salt and freshly ground black pepper

Cut the tomatoes in half, and slice thinly. Then take the carrots, peel and grate them coarsly, and also peel the cucumber, remove the seeds, cut in half and slice thinly. Cut the tuna into small squares of about 2.5cm (1in). Place the tomato, carrots, cucumber, white onion, ginger and lime juice in a bowl and mix. Place the tuna in a separate bowl, add the vinegar, salt and pepper, mix well and cure for 45 seconds—the colour of the meat should turn white. Add the tuna to the vegetable mixture and mix well, before finally adding the coconut milk. To serve, place in small bowls.

Serves 10

Hawaiian Chicken

1 large can of pineapple slices
1 large sweet onion sliced
3 chicken breasts split in half
½ can peach jam
1 tbsp soy sauce
1 tbsp olive oil
1 tbsp white wine vinegar
1 red capsicum

Drain pineapple from the can and set aside. Sprinkle chicken with salt.
Brown the chicken in a frying pan in the olive oil, then add the onions
and green pepper, cover and cook. In a bowl, mix the jam, soy sauce and
vinegar, the pour over chicken and cook about three minutes. Take the
chicken off the heat and place on a serving platter. Add the pineapple to
the sauce, and heat thoroughly. To serve, place the pineapple on top of
the chicken, and spoon the sauce all over. Serve with white rice, and your
choice of steamed vegetables.

Serves six

tralasia Australasia

06:

Australasia

*I*t's a part of the world that's associated with exotic wildlife and mystical landscapes, and the island nations of Australia and New Zealand co-exist in the South Pacific as close neighbours with completely different personalities.

On one side of the Tasman Sea, it's the vast and ethereal Outback with kangaroos, emus, crocodiles, colourful parrots and koala bears, and on the other it's the soaring snow capped mountain peaks and beautiful valleys as seen in the three *Lord of the Rings* movies. Australia and New Zealand, collectively known as Australasia, are the proverbial odd couple with at least a few things in common. Tens of thousands of kilometres of unspoiled beaches frame both countries and their people possess a laid-back demeanour which becomes contagious for many visitors.

They seem to revel in their geographic isolation, although in recent years the sharp increase in cruise ship numbers in the region indicates that the rest of the world wants to see and experience both countries. With attractive and cosmopolitan cities, charming country towns and cuisine that's as fresh and unique as the destinations, Australasia is a beguiling place that has a lasting impact on those fortunate enough to sail its waters.

New Zealand

The early Polynesian inhabitants called their home Aotearoa, meaning 'The Land of the Long White Cloud', and since European traders and whalers arrived in the late 18th century, it's a country which has retained a reputation as a ruggedly beautiful and mysterious place. New Zealand is a land of geysers and glaciers, and at its modern heart is a fascinating fusion of a strong Maori culture and a distinct bond with its colonial past, thanks to settlement by the British in the early 19th century. Maori settlement preceded the Europeans by around 1,000 years. This culture has common links with Polynesians from the Cook Islands, Hawai`i and Tahiti, and has a strong influence on the daily lives of all New Zealanders, including the Pakeha, or locals of European ancestry.

The country is neatly packaged up in two parts, the North Island and the South Island, with Cook Strait separating them by 20km at its narrowest point. In general terms the North Island is more heavily populated with bigger cities including Auckland and the capital Wellington, while the South Island is the 'star of the show' in New Zealand with its spectacular mountains, lakes and glaciers. From the Bay of Islands at the top of the North Island to Fiordland in the South Island, cruising New Zealand opens up a world of natural wonders and reveals a vibrant culture which really defines a proud nation.

THE SOUTH ISLAND

It's six-thirty in the morning in late November, and even though it's almost summer, the temperature has just nudged above freezing and an icy wind rips across the deck as something of a wake-me-up for the people who obeyed their alarm clocks to brave the elements. The sheer mountains all around block the sun and funnel the wind, but as the ship enters the glassy waters of Milford Sound, the landscape which emerges becomes the primary focus and everyone forgets just how cold it is.

Surrounding the ship is an untouched wilderness with towering mountains dropping straight into the fiord, where icy water pours off the hillsides to form dramatic waterfalls, and where jagged, snow-capped peaks tear through the clouds in search of sunlight. Located on the south-west coast of the South Island, Milford Sound is part of a stunning alpine region called Fiordland, a World Heritage Area which defines New Zealand's worldwide image as a place blessed with a flawless and mystical physical beauty. Fiordland is mostly contained within the Fiordland National Park, and at just over 12,000 square kilometres, it's the largest national park in New Zealand and one of the most uninhabited places in the world. Most of Fiordland is inaccessible except by ship or air because of the extreme nature of the terrain created by glacial movement during the last ice age more than 15,000 years ago.

Milford Sound, at the very top of Fiordland, is a 15 kilometre stretch of narrow water which starts in the Tasman Sea and winds inland past mountains that rise to between 1,000 and 1,200 metres on each side with forests clinging precariously to the cliff faces. Dolphins, seals and penguins also frequent the calm waters of Milford Sound and add to the 'other-world' feeling of the place, along with the calls of some of the strangest birds in the world from the forests including the world's only mountain parrot, the kea, which are seen frequently flying around Milford Sound.

Of the 14 fiords in Fiordland, Doubtful Sound to the south of the national park is the largest, about three times longer than Milford Sound with three distinct arms. It's a labyrinth of waterways surrounded by steep mountain cliffs which are serene and peaceful, yet overwhelming, and it's easy to see how film producers were inspired to create their model Tolkien's Middle Earth. The former New Zealand Governor-General Charles John Lyttelton (1957-1962) reportedly said of the region: 'This is big country. One day peaceful, a study in green and blue, the next melancholy and misty, with low cloud veiling the tops, an awesome place, with its granite precipices, its hanging valleys, its earthquake faults and its thundering cascades.'

FIORD OR SOUND?

New Zealand's Fiordland is one of the most picturesque wilderness regions on the planet, and home of the stunning Milford and Dusky Sounds. In Maori legend, these inspiring fiords were created by Tu-te-raki-whanoa, a demi-god who came wielding a magical adze and uttering incantations. In the scientific world, however, they were created by rivers of ice, and are actually named incorrectly. Throughout Fiordland the fiords are officially mapped as sounds, but strictly speaking, they should be called fiords. So what's the difference? A fiord is a narrow glaciated valley with steep sides, which has been flooded by the sea after the glacier's retreat. In contrast, a sound is a river valley flooded by the sea following a rise in sea levels, a depression of the land, or a combination of both. Located at the mountainous northern end of Fiordland National Park, Milford Sound is classed as a classic fiord. It's a deep water inlet straddled by steep mountains, one of which is the famous Mitre Peak.

Cruising the South Island is an exercise that involves scenery of a grand scale and the towns and cities possess a relaxed and often understated charm which provides a contrast to the spectacular landscapes. Dunedin, the South Island's second biggest city with a population of just over 120,000, is a real throwback to New Zealand's colonial heritage with Scottish Edwardian architecture scattered around its streets. The city was founded in 1848 mainly because of its natural harbour and was given the name New Edinburgh, which was eventually changed to a version of the old Celtic name for the famous Scottish city, Dun Edin. The Scottish migrants that founded the settlement probably had little idea they were to create New Zealand's biggest and most important city, for a time at least, as the discovery of gold in 1861 ensured Dunedin became the commercial and industrial hub for the country. The influx of migrants and resulting economic wealth led to the construction of much of the grand architecture in the city today including St Paul's Cathedral, Dunedin Railway Station and the Town Hall. Today these impressive buildings are the heart and soul of the city, which seems proud of its history although it's certainly not mired in its past glories. When the gold ran out, the cities on the North Island took over as New Zealand's major centres and these days Dunedin is a university town with around 10% of its student population now driving the economy and cultural activities.

Christchurch, further to the north, has a similar youthful exuberance although this is a distinctly 'English' city on the surface. It's the biggest city on the South Island, although it's a calm and laid-back place, and it's here that the narrow Avon River meanders through grassy river banks lined with willow trees, beautiful gardens and stately buildings. Young gentlemen from the Edwardian era (local students) push punts through the tranquil setting for the romantically inclined and this could easily be a snapshot of a languid summer's afternoon in Oxford or Cambridge. Away from the river Gothic style buildings dominate the skyline with Christchurch Cathedral on Cathedral Square in the city centre towering over arguably New Zealand's most beautiful city. The downtown itself is a haven for pedestrians with parks and gardens linking up with shops, cafés, bars and restaurants, while beautifully restored trams travel on a two and a half kilometre loop of the city and surrounds, taking in all the main attractions including the Botanic Gardens, which have the best examples of New Zealand's indigenous plants set against the backdrop of sweeping lawns and lakes.

THE NORTH ISLAND

It's the smell you first notice as you enter Rotorua. It's that familiar rotten egg odour which logic tells you is sulphur and perfectly natural, especially for an area renowned for its geothermal activity, but it does take some time to adjust and become used to it. Around the town, clouds of steam and gas rise up as if to confirm that this is quite literally one of the hottest tourist destinations in New Zealand. While the South Island receives most of the accolades for its natural wonders, the geothermal activity of Rotorua, which produces stunning geysers, steaming hot springs and bubbling mud pools, has been one of the country's most popular tourist destinations since the early 1800s. Known as Sulphur City, it's located in the Bay of Plenty region about 60 kilometres south of the cruise ship port of Tauranga, an attractive surfie town in its own right. Of the several geysers in the area, the star attraction is the lively Pohutu geyser, a crowd-pleaser which erupts around 20 times a day, shooting a deadly combination of water and steam into the air, sometimes as high as 30 metres. Pohutu is in the Whakarewarewa Thermal Village which is a cultural centre built around its spectacular geysers and mud pools and there's also daily cultural performances by the local Tuhourangi-Ngati Wahiao people, who've lived in the area for more than 200 years. In traditional dress, the local men perform the famous warrior dance, the *haka*, while the women's *poi* dance with ball and twine is another Maori tradition which is faithfully brought to life.

BELOW: Cruising off the east coast of the North Island

This is an area of stunning beauty where the traditional culture of the Maori is proudly maintained. Legend has it that the Te Arawa people from Eastern Polynesia originally settled the Rotorua area in the 14th century and they began hosting people in the early 1800s as New Zealand's first tourism venture. The geothermal spectacle, along with the 16 lakes in the region, creates a world of unique beauty and it's also become one of the great adventure destinations in the country. From hiking to horse riding, mountain biking, jet boating, bungy jumping, white water rafting, sky diving and four wheel driving, Rotorua's reputation as one of the world's most exciting cruise destinations is well deserved.

While Rotorua has remained an enduring location for more than 200 years thanks to its unique natural attributes, the cities of the North Island have really emerged as cosmopolitan and worldly places in the past decade or so. The nation's capital, Wellington, at the bottom of the North Island is the geographic centre of New Zealand, but it's spent most of its life well and truly in the shadow of the likes of Auckland, Christchurch, Queenstown and Rotorua. These days it's laying claim to being the 'hippest' place in New Zealand and with good reason, and not just because several glossy style magazines have proclaimed it so. Set against the backdrop of a mountain that drops quite dramatically into the ocean, with terrace houses perched on the slope, Wellington has been called the 'San Francisco of the Southern Hemisphere', and while this may be a little fanciful it does give the place an attractive physical aspect that most cities simply don't have. Its cultural delights, of which there are many, belie the fact that this is a city that's out to have some fun.

The café, restaurant and bar scene is decidedly sophisticated and for a relatively small city (population 170,000) there's an awful lot of them concentrated in a very walkable CBD. Of the 300 or so eateries in Wellington the majority feature contemporary cuisine with a Pacific Rim style that fuses the best local produce such as seafood, lamb and beef with Chinese, Asian and increasingly, Mediterranean influences. Well and truly gone are the days when New Zealand was something of a 'meat-and-two-veg' type of place with fish and chips and bland Chinese food as the options and a short wander through the streets of Wellington reveals just how far the culinary scene has evolved. Japanese, Thai, Indian, Malaysian, French, Italian and Middle Eastern restaurants jostle for attention and deliver authentic dishes and in the homes of the city dwellers in particular, variations of these themes are increasingly being served on the table. This evolution began two decades ago when Kiwis started travelling the world in increased numbers, returning home to demand more cosmopolitan options, and when immigration restrictions were eased in 1987. With this buzz in Wellington, it seems there's a party happening downtown on most nights of the week, with Monday night perhaps an exception, and during the day culture vultures have a swathe of museums and galleries including New Zealand's best, the Te Papa Tongarewa Museum, which is the national museum showcasing the unique heritage of the country covering art, history and its heritage.

Australia

From the Great Barrier Reef in the tropical north, to its subantarctic islands in the south, Australia's landscape and seascape combine to form a mélange of natural wonders, unique wildlife, cosmopolitan cities and quaint country towns. Although the 'Land Down Under' is famed for its wide open spaces and the Outback of vast desert plains, it is in fact a highly urbanised nation. In modern Australia the cityscapes are becoming tourist attractions in their own right, and this is a place where you can snorkel with colourful tropical fish and coral, ski through eucalypt trees, ride a camel through a desert, sip espresso in a cozy café, catch a wave at a spectacular beach or just sit in a bar and chat with the locals. All the tourist clichés which have made Australia famous are still there—the Opera House, Sydney Harbour Bridge, Bondi Beach and Uluru (formerly Ayers Rock)—but there's more to this continent than a handful of iconic landmarks. It's a young country with a fresh approach to life and this is reflected in the cuisine which, like New Zealand, is a blend of the Pacific Rim style with European and Asian influences, along with authentic food styles from around the world. Its wines have also gained international acclaim, and with inexpensive prices this is a major drawcard for many visitors and one of the reasons Australia is one of the world's most popular cruise destinations.

European settlement began in 1788 with the establishment of a British penal colony, but the vast majority of immigrants were free settlers and the modern culture of Australia remains a reflection of its British origins. Aboriginal culture, which began 40,000 years ago, was largely eliminated as a result of European colonisation and the population was cut dramatically because of the introduction of western diseases such as smallpox. Today around 3per cent of the population is of Aboriginal origin, and the Aboriginal rights movement enjoys a growing public support for its causes.

THE GREAT BARRIER REEF

You're in the middle of the high seas, around 30 kilometres from the mainland with no land or other vessels in sight, and it's time to jump into the azure blue water. You hit the water, give the 'okay' sign, and head towards the expanse of reef. It's only a few metres away and the reef edge drops into the deep blue and after a few more kicks you're over the coral. That's when the overwhelming beauty of the Great Barrier Reef kicks in. Colourful corals of all sizes, pretty reef fish, giant clams, starfish and the odd small shark combine in a show of nature which is simply breathtaking. There are many ways to experience the Barrier Reef, including day-trips on boats and flights in planes or helicopters, but cruising this spectacular natural phenomenon puts you right amongst all it has to offer above and below water, and it's a good way to avoid the crowds that often result from day-trip operations.

Cruising offers serious divers, first-timer divers, snorkeling enthusiasts, and sightseers a more in-depth and leisurely way to explore more of the reef's picturesque sides and natural charms. They include tiny coral cays, small islands teeming with unique plants and wildlife, historical sites, and the various pockets of the inner and outer reef itself. Many of them feature different coral formations and marine life, and some cannot be accessed by day-trippers. The Great Barrier Reef is one of the Seven Natural Wonders of the World and is also a World Heritage Site. It's the world's largest coral reef system comprised of

3,000 individual reefs and 900 islands which stretch along the coast of Queensland for more than 2,500 kilometres and it's no wonder it can be seen from outer space. The world's largest structure built by living organisms, the Barrier Reef is regularly rated the number one reason to visit Australia.

Within the Great Barrier Reef, one island group in particular stands out as the ultimate cruise destination, and the Whitsundays is one of those places that on the surface seems too good to be true. Think for a minute about what would constitute the perfect tropical island getaway: warm weather, calm azure waters, blinding white sand beaches, colourful marine life and corals, and hammocks overlooking the water. Throw in cocktail bars, unreal sunsets, sailing boats and all manner of water sports and you have the Whitsunday Islands in a nutshell, a 74-island group in North Queensland which has been widely described as the most beautiful place on earth. For sheer romance, it's pretty hard to beat, and the moment you cruise into its waters, you know this is somewhere a bit special.

Cruising the region reveals the true beauty of this part of the Great Barrier Reef, which is widely regarded as the most visually spectacular part of the system. In among the lush green islands that meet the blue ocean, all manner of tours and activities are possible off ship and the main problem is resisting the urge to do it all. From snorkeling and scuba diving, to sailing, whale watching, reef fishing, riding in a helicopter, water skiing, jet skiing, parasailing, sea kayaking, hiking in rain forests, fish feeding, picnicking on secluded beaches, and playing tennis, it's an adventure destination that caters for all tastes, but there's no shame in sitting on the deck of a ship with cocktail in hand to catch a few rays and watch everyone else indulge in the active pursuits.

NAVIGATING THE REEF

If you are lucky enough to be invited onto the bridge of a modern-day cruise ship, you could be forgiven for thinking you stepped into a futuristic space ship. Forget any concepts of an old fashioned ship's steering wheel. Today's modern liners are fitted with multi-million-dollar state-of-the-art technology including impressive navigation equipment which allows their captains to navigate some of the most treacherous and difficult waterways on the planet. Australia's Great Barrier Reef is one such region where seafarers have sailed at their peril including the great Captain James Cook. Between May and August in 1770, Cook's *Endeavour* navigated the full length of the Great Barrier Reef. And although most of the voyage was made well inshore, probably allowing its crew to see little of the Reef, on 11 June *Endeavour* became intimately acquainted with it when it struck what's now called Endeavour Reef, north of Cape Tribulation.

Due to this unforeseen mishap, the crew of *Endeavour* were forced to spend six weeks ashore, repairing the ship at the site we know today as the settlement of Cooktown.

Also, as a result, Cook, his scientists, and a staff of four illustrators were unable to carry out very much direct scientific observation of the Reef. But as a result of *Endeavour*'s voyage, and the unexpected encounter, the international scientific community would soon know that it existed and that it was impressive in size. The story then goes that after all the repairs were carried out, Cook decided to head for the open ocean, but could not find a way through the Reef. In a desperate attempt to get back on track, he sailed north to what we know as Lizard Island. There, he climbed the island at its highest point, and was able to see a break in the Reef large enough for the *Endeavour* to pass through. This break became known as Cook's Passage.

RIGHT: Seven Seas Mariner docked at Circular Quay, Sydney

NEXT PAGE
LEFT: Surfers Paradise, Queensland's Gold Coast
RIGHT ABOVE: Sydney Harbour Bridge at night
RIGHT BELOW: Flinders Street Station, Melbourne

MAINLAND AUSTRALIA

Along with Hong Kong, Sydney often rates as the top destination for world cruisers and the primary reason is the expansive harbour that runs right through the heart of Australia's largest city. Sailing into, or out of, Sydney Harbour is one of those experiences which creates a lifelong impression. From the moment you turn and sail through Sydney Heads, the stunning natural harbour helps form a cityscape without comparison. Granite cliffs and national parks rise up from the water and dotted among the vegetation are homes of the people fortunate enough to live here. On the harbour itself, ferries charge around carrying commuters and visitors to the numerous suburbs and water front villages, and competition sailing boats and pleasure craft somehow mingle comfortably in the setting. The centrepiece of all this is the Sydney Harbour Bridge and Opera House, which combine to create one of the most photographed landscapes in the world. Most cruise ships dock in Circular Quay, which is literally between the two tourist icons, and it provides an uninterrupted view of the most famous man-made structures in this region.

Like most of Australia's other major cities, Sydney is a cosmopolitan place with a fresh 'new world' approach which has become a favourite destination for foodies from around the world. With literally thousands of restaurants spread throughout the downtown and suburbs, it's the type of place where you can dine in a sophisticated environment with food prepared by a celebrity chef or simply sit down at a plastic table with a bowl of authentic noodles in a busy hole-in-the-wall joint. Sydney's reputation as the culinary capital of Australia is constantly under challenge from its southern neighbour Melbourne, and the country's second biggest city has good reason to be miffed when the Harbour City grabs all the attention.

Melbourne may have the Yarra River as its lifeblood instead of a harbour, but this busy city features one of the most culturally diverse communities in the world with residents from more than 140 nations and this is reflected in the range of eateries which easily matches that of Sydney. In the inner suburbs in particular, Thai, Vietnamese, Chinese, Indian, Italian and Greek restaurants seem as commonplace as the ubiquitous corner store and scattered throughout the city are family-run establishments from other parts of Asia, Europe, the Middle East and Africa. Like New Zealand, Pacific Rim cuisine, influenced by the multicultural surroundings, dominates the top end restaurants in Sydney and Melbourne, and the country's other state capitals have also embraced this eclectic style of dining, along with a noticeable Mediterranean-style café culture. Brisbane, Adelaide, Perth and Darwin each have a unique and vibrant atmosphere and an appealing cityscape, which makes strolling their streets a relaxing and pleasant experience.

UNIQUELY AUSTRALIAN

For more than 40,000 years, aboriginal Australians have carried on a shared tradition of cultural and sacred knowledge, known as the Dreamtime. It's the story of the relationship between humankind and the earth, the story of creation, and a story of how to live in harmony with one another and our environment. In recent years, however, elements of this indigenous culture and use of native ingredients have emerged in the mainstream of cuisine. Indigenous ingredients are key elements of Australian native dishes - a style of cooking which has come under the spotlight in recent years, and the benefits of some indigenous ingredients extend beyond their unique flavours.

Kakadu Plum: it contains the world's highest amount of natural vitamin C, and in cooking it's used as a garnish.

Wild Rosella Flower: it's high in natural phenols which protect the skin from free radical damage. In cooking, however, it's a delicious ingredient which can be used in sauces, pie fillings, pastries, ice-cream, or as a garnish.

Alpine Pepper: it increases circulation and warms muscles, and can be used to season meats or vegetables.

Lemon Myrtle: has a high content of Citrol, which has antibacterial properties. The oil is used for cooking.

Quandong: the fruit can be used in sauces or as a garnish, and the kernel oil is a natural anti-inflammatory.

Bush Tomato: used in chutneys and sauces.

Lemon Aspen Fruit and Juice: the fruit is used as a garnish, the juice to flavour desserts, dressings and sauces.

Munthari: a fruit used in muffins, fruit pies, puddings, or sautéd with onions or mushrooms

Wattleseed: used in desserts and baked products.

Forest Peppermint: used in desserts, especially ice-cream.

TASMANIA

Separated from the Australian mainland by the 240km (150 mile) stretch of Bass Strait, Tasmania looks like it was added on to the south-east corner as something of an afterthought, and until recently it was overlooked as a major cruise ship destination. These days most Australasian itineraries include at least one port of call in the 'Apple Isle' and the reason is quite simple: rolling green hills that sweep down to beautiful beaches, rugged mountains, meandering river streams, world class cool climate wineries, and a genuine laid-back island mentality that becomes very easy to adopt. Almost 40 per cent of Tasmania is made up of World Heritage Sites, national parks and nature reserves, and it's a combination of beautiful scenery and strong colonial heritage. In the early 1800s, Tasmania was settled as a British penal colony when it was known as Van Diemen's Land, and today much of the original architecture from that period remains intact in the towns which have sprung up in their place.

Hobart, the capital city of the state of Tasmania, was the site of one of the penal colonies and this is where most cruise ships dock when they head to the island. As you sail up the Derwent River, it's obvious this is a city with strong maritime roots, with fishing, sailing and tour boats increasing in numbers the closer you get to Hobart. The city itself is set right on a beautiful harbour, which is really just a wide section of the Derwent, and it has the imposing Mount Wellington at 1270 metres (4,000ft) as a dramatic backdrop. The 21km (13 mile) drive from Hobart to the summit takes in the temperate rainforest and sub-alpine flora and ends in breathtaking, panoramic views of Hobart, Bruny Island, South Arm and the Tasman Peninsula. It's a snapshot of Tasmania only, and confirms the fact that this is a place that could take months at least to even partially explore.

BELOW: Constitution Dock, Hobart

CHEFS AT SEA, BENJAMIN CHRISTIE

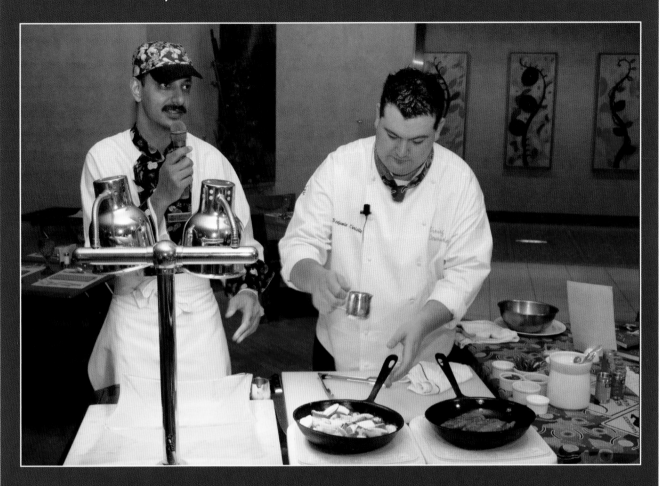

The Australian chef, Benjamin Christie, is one of an elite group of guest chefs who makes regular appearances on board the ships of Regent Seven Seas Cruises during the Australasian season. Christie, who hails from Sydney, is widely regarded as a culinary ambassador for Australia, and co-hosted the popular television series Dining Downunder with Vic Cherikoff. His first experience of luxury cruising was on board Regent's Seven Seas Mariner in 2005. Christie and Cherikoff were on board to present two gala dinners and two cooking classes showcasing Australian cuisine. It was a five-day crossing from Hobart to Melbourne which left the Aussie chef with fond memories.

'I had never cruised before, but I had always wanted to try it out so I jumped at the chance when I was invited. One of the gala dinners featured kangaroo, sparking curiosity among the ship's mainly North American guests, and while they were keen to try it, as every chef knows, handling this Aussie game meat can be tricky. Kangaroo is best served medium-rare and immediately, and having it come out of a ship's kitchen in large quantities, and then being held in bays waiting to be served to guests created a few issues. Cooking classes on cruise ships are a really big thing today. One of ours attracted 110 guests, and I think it was because the cooking we were showing them was completely different. There are lots of new flavours out there that people know nothing about, and when it comes to Australian cuisine, what they think is a very primitive way of cooking turns out to be just as contemporary as something you'd get at a top restaurant in the States. As for cruising I really enjoyed the experience, and I also developed a new respect for cruise ship staff. I thought I worked hard, but those guys have to work incredibly hard and very long hours every day.'

Cocktails

Pink Angel

3 parts white rum
1½ parts Advocaat
2 parts cream
1½ parts Cherry Liqueur
1 egg white

Pour all ingredients into a cocktail shaker with ice,
shake and strain into a cocktail or martini glass and serve.

Kiwi Bellini

1 part 42 Below Kiwi Vodka
½ ripe green kiwifruit, peeled
Champagne or sparkling wine

Mash or puree the kiwifruit, and press through a sieve to remove
the black seeds. Add the vodka, and spoon the puree into a champagne
glass. Then add champagne or sparkling wine, mix gently, and serve.

RIGHT: Pink Angel

Recipes

Cauliflower Soup with Marron, Lemon Myrtle & Paperbark Smoked Oil

(Provided by Chef Benjamin Christie)

2 cauliflowers
500g (1.1lbs)potatoes
2 tsp butter
200g (7oz) diced onions
200g (7oz) diced potatoes
50g (1¾oz) blonde roux (if required)
2lt (4.2 pints) prawn stock
250ml (1 cup) cream
2 tsp salt
2 tsp lemon myrtle sprinkle
500g (1lb) poached marron tails
20ml (½fl oz) Paperbark smoked Oil

Clean and chop the cauliflower, and peel and dice potatoes. In a saucepan, melt a little butter, sauté the onions and add the cauliflower. Add prawn stock and potatoes, bring to the boil, and simmer for 60 minutes. Meanwhile, take the poached marron tails, remove the shells and thinly slice across the tails. After the soup has simmered, remove from the heat, add cream, season with Outback salt and blend. If required add blonde roux to thicken.

Immediately before serving, add a sprinkle of lemon myrtle to the soup. Pour into bowls, and serve with approximately 50g of marron tail, and a drizzle of paperbark smoked oil on top.

Serves approximately ten

Kangaroo Fillet with Yakajirri Rosti

(Provided by Chef Benjamin Christie)

4 × 120g (4oz) kangaroo fillet
2 tbsp mountain pepper sauce
8 quandong confit halves
1 punnet shitake mushrooms
1 punnet oyster mushrooms
1 punnet enoki mushrooms
60ml (2fl oz) chicken jus
pinch forest anise
pinch of salt
80g (2½oz) corn flour
1 tbsp butter

Yakajirri Rosti:
1 tsp Yakajirri
750g (1.6lb) Idaho potatoes
1 large egg
2 tbsp corn flour or corn starch
2 shallots, finely chopped
pinch of salt
1 tbsp butter

Begin by marinating the kangaroo fillet in the mountain pepper sauce, cover and refrigerate.

For the Yakajirri rosti, start by peeling the potatoes, then grate into a bowl. Squeeze the grated potato of any liquid, and combine with yakajirri, egg, corn flour, shallots and salt. On a hotplate or skillet, melt a little butter on medium heat. Using egg rings, place a little of the yakajirri potato mixture into each one. Seal both sides, and place on baking tray. When all are sealed off, bake the rosti in the oven at 170°C (340°F) until well browned.

Season the kangaroo fillet with salt and sear on a grill to medium rare. Cook each side for about 4 minutes, then remove and allow to rest in a warm place. Separately, prepare the enoki mushrooms by breaking them apart, dust in corn flour and deep fry till golden. Remove and allow to drain on a paper towel.

While the kangaroo fillet is resting, melt a little butter in a saucepan and sauté the shitake and oyster mushrooms. Deglaze with chicken jus, then season with forest anise and allow to simmer.

To serve, slice the kangaroo fillet across the grain. Place the rosti on the plate with the kangaroo on top, garnish with the enoki mushrooms and two quandong halves, then drizzle the prepared mushroom sauce around the edge of the plate.

Serves four

Crumbed Chilli Baby Octopus with Rocket

1 kg (2.2lb) of baby octopus, gutted and cleaned
1lt (2.1 pints) vegetable stock
300ml (10fl oz) white wine
juice of one lemon
flour for dusting
a large bunch of rocket salad, trimmed and washed

Marinade
250ml (8.5fl oz) olive oil
100 ml (3.4fl oz) balsamic vinegar
100 ml (3.4fl oz) sweet chilli sauce
50ml (1.7fl oz) white wine
5 cloves of garlic, crushed
freshly ground black pepper

In a saucepan, bring the stock, wine and lemon juice to the boil, add
the octopus and simmer gently until tender. Drain and cool. Mix all the
marinade ingredients together, pour over the cooked octopus and stand
for at least three hours (preferably overnight in the fridge). When ready to
cook, add olive oil to a frying pan and heat until very hot. Dust the octopus
lightly in the flour, and sear in the olive oil until crispy. Serve with rocket
leaves drizzled in olive oil.

Serves four

Lamingtons

Australia's national cake, made popular by a former Governor of Queensland, Lord Lamington.

3 eggs
½ cup castor sugar
¾ cup self-raising flour
¼ cup cornflour
15g (½oz) butter
3 tbsp hot water
3 cups desiccated coconut

Icing
500g (1lb) icing sugar
$1/3$ cup of cocoa
15g (½oz) of butter
½ cup of milk

Beat the eggs until creamy, gradually add the sugar and beat until sugar is completely dissolved. Fold in sifted flour and cornflour, then the combined water and butter.

Pour mixture into prepared baking tins of about 18cm x 28cm (7in x 11in), and bake in moderate oven for approximately half an hour. Once cooked, cool on a wire rack.

Sift the icing sugar and cocoa into heatproof bowl. Stir in butter and milk, and stir over a pan of hot water until icing is smooth and glossy. Trim the brown top and sides from the cake, and cut into 16 even pieces. Dip each piece of cake into the icing, hold over the bowl to drain off excess chocolate, and coat in the coconut.

Serves 16

RIGHT: Hobart from Mt. Wellington
ABOVE: Sydney city and harbour from the air

Mexico & The Caribbean

07:
Mexico &
The Caribbean

Exotic, colourful, and diverse are just three of the many words which could be used in an attempt to describe the essence and spirit of these two hugely popular cruising regions. Although they are geographic neighbours, aside from a tropical location in the Americas, it's there that the similarities end. In Mexico, you have a vast nation bordered by the United States in the north, and Central America in the south, and flanked by two of the world's great oceans, the Pacific in the west, and the Caribbean Sea in the east. Orderly and chaotic in the same breath, Mexico is a country which overwhelms the senses on many levels; from sights and sounds to tastes and smells, it's a unique and intoxicating mix of cultures and landscape. In contrast, the Caribbean is an impressive archipelago of more than 7,000 islands, islets, reefs and cays, which stretch for over 4,020 kilometres or 2,500 miles. And thanks to a rich, colourful, and often torrid history, it's a region which hasn't embraced a single culture, but instead is a complex fusion of African, British, French, Dutch, Indian and Spanish heritage, brought from the homelands of past foreign settlers. Each island not only has its own geography and unique qualities, but also a cultural flavour.

Mexico

If Mexico were a person, it would be fair to describe it as having an engaging multiple personality disorder. The northern part of the country is characterised by its deserts and rugged mountain ranges while, in contrast, the southern states are lined with the shores of the Pacific Ocean and Gulf of Mexico, with an abundance of mangrove swamps and forests. And then there's central Mexico, the heartland of the country dotted with picturesque and colourful towns, villages and colonial cities, some of which have been declared World Heritage Sites. For most travellers who visit by ship, however, their experience of Mexico is limited to a variety of destinations on the Pacific Coast and the Yucatan Peninsula. Both areas of grand natural beauty, exotic marine life, and stunning beaches, they are not lacking in either colour or history and possess a unique character of their own.

THE PACIFIC COAST

From the steamy craziness of Acapulco and the hedonists' delight of Cabo San Lucas, to the shabby chic of Mazatlan and pristine beaches of Huatulco, cruising the Pacific Coast of Mexico reveals an eclectic mix of exotic destinations. From south to north the landscape changes, then changes again. All along, the coastline is dotted with communities, from tiny fishing villages to major resort destinations, and everything in between. In the south, the state of Oaxaca is known for its important history and culture, and it's also the site of one of the country's newest eco-friendly resort areas, the Bahias de Huatulco, or Bays of Huatulco. A collection of nine bays and 36 beaches along a rugged 35 kilometre or 22 mile coastline, Huatulco is a beach and ocean lovers' paradise unspoiled by modern commercial tourism so far, and surprisingly it doesn't even rate a mention on many maps. But it's a place which boasts a backdrop of the Sierra Madre mountains, and one where you can find a secluded white sand beach, abundant marine life, and enjoy the flavour of a real Mexican village in the nearby inland village of La Crucecita.

Around 600 kilometres or 373 miles further north is the best-known resort on Mexico's Pacific coastline, if not the entire country. Acapulco is a city which thrived in the 1950s thanks to the Hollywood jetset; an era when Frank Sinatra invited one and all to 'Come fly with me...down to Acapulco Bay,' and Elvis Presley spread the message in the early 1960s with his hit film *Fun in Acapulco*. Today Acapulco remains a modern-day playground for the rich and famous, thanks to its sweeping bay, stunning beaches dotted with tall, majestic palm trees, its history, and a manic energy. One of the city's enduring traditions is performed by its famous gang of cliff divers, who've earned a reputation around the world for their daring. From a height of 40 metres or over 130 feet at the famous cliffs of *La Quebrada*, just north of the Old Town, the divers risk their lives with each leap. The skill and timing of the divers has been a major drawcard for Acapulco for decades, and for good reason.

To the north of Acapulco, Mazatlan exudes a colonial charm which mirrors its rise to prominence as an influential port city in the early 1800s, and it can claim to be ahead of Acapulco in that it began a tourism industry in the early 1900s, thanks to its year-round perfect weather and nice beaches. Like many Mexican port cities there are two distinct sides of Mazatlan. One is the *malecon*, or seaside boulevard which stretches for more than 16 kilometres past golden sands and good surf breaks. And there's an Old Town, and at the heart of Old Mazatlan is the *Plaza de la Republica*. Facing the plaza is the *Catedral de Inmaculada Concepcion* (Cathedral of the Immaculate Conception) which was built in the late 1800s and serves as a useful landmark with its distinctive yellow-tiled spires.

The crossing from Mazatlan to Cabo San Lucas over the Gulf of California can be a bumpy experience, as it's a spot where the cold currents of the north clash with the warmer ones from the south. But the reward is a Mexican seaside resort which is becoming one of the most popular destinations in this part of the world. On the southern tip of Baja California, Cabo San Lucas is a beach lovers' paradise with a nightlife that's become legendary. Blessed with great weather and warm water year-round, the reasons for visiting Cabo are varied, but they all revolve around enjoying the great outdoors. Sun worshippers, party animals, divers, snorkelers, surfers, fishing enthusiasts and golfers hit Cabo to indulge their past-time during the day, and it all makes for an amusing mix of people when the sun goes down and it's time to go out and play. The most popular beach is *Playa El Médano*, just east of the marina, and although it's often quite busy, it is a beautiful stretch of pure white sand and azure water. A quieter and more beautiful option is *Playa del Amor*, or Lovers' Beach, which is on the western side of the marina. The most famous landmark in Cabo, however, are the stunning rock formations called *Los Arcos*, which rise up out of the Sea of Cortez and provide the perfect backdrop for a Mexican sunset.

CHILLIES....A MEXICAN LOVE AFFAIR

Mexican food varies greatly by region, in part because of the local climate and geography, but also as a result of ethnic differences among the indigenous inhabitants. In fact, Mexico's food has a long and diverse history with many influences, particularly from the Spanish after they invaded the country in 1521. But one ingredient which is synonymous with Mexican cuisine is the chilli pepper. Chillies are the fruit of a plant, not a vegetable, and according to historians they have been a part of the human diet in Mexico since at least 7000 BC. They belong to the same family of plants as capsicums, and their use in cuisine is as a spice. One of the first Europeans to have encountered chillies was Christopher Columbus in the Caribbean. After this time they were cultivated around the globe, and from Mexico they spread rapidly into the Philippines, and then to India, China, Korea and Japan, and were incorporated into local cuisines.

There are said to be more than 100 different types of chilli peppers, and common varieties include paprika, cayenne, jalapeños, and the tabasco peppers which make the self-titled sauce. In addition to being exciting to eat, they actually have some health benefits. They are high in Vitamin C, an antioxidant which may help protect against cancer, the capsaicin (the predominant ingredient in chilli), is an anticoagulant, which may help to prevent heart attacks or strokes caused by blood clots. As any chilli devotee knows, generally a smaller chilli means a hotter chilli. But what can you do if you eat a pepper which proves to be too hot for your palette? One remedy which some people swear by is drinking tomato juice or eating the fruit of a fresh lemon or lime. Others claim that drinking milk will do the trick, or chewing on rice or bread.

THE YUCATAN PENINSULA

This steamy region of Mexico lies in the southeastern corner of the country, between the Gulf of Mexico and the Caribbean Sea. Boasting a year-round hot and humid climate, it's a haven of beach resorts and natural paradises. The peninsula comprises three states—Campeche, Yucatan and Quintana Roo—and is famous for being the home of many Mayan archeological sites. Here, visitors discover that many of the traditions of the Maya persist, from the traditional blouse worn by women called a huipil, to the homes with straw rooftops. Destinations which are popular for visitors include Campeche, an historic commercial port and fortified city which is also a World Heritage site, and the nearby archeological zones, Edzna and Calakmul. Two hours away is the white city of Merida, famous for its local cuisine, historical buildings, and freshwater pools which connect to a network of amazing submerged caverns. Here you will also discover the two most cherished ancient sites of the Mayan world, Chichen Itza and Uxmal.

On the Mayan Riviera in Quintana Roo, there are the stunning ecological parks of Xcaret and Xel-Ha, as well as the Great Mayan Reef, the second largest reef in the world, and a paradise for scuba diving and snorkelling. Major drawcards of the region are its beaches and famous beach resorts, and a few of the most popular ones, including Cancun, Cozumel, Isla Mujeres and Playa del Carmen feature on many Caribbean cruise itineraries. Cancun vies with Acapulco for the number-one best-known Mexican resort. A mini-metropolis on the Mayan Riviera, its impressive beachfront hotel strip stretches for more than 30 kilometres or 19 miles and is packed with hotels, spas, shopping malls and restaurants. But Cancun also boasts a year-round subtropical climate which keeps visitors returning, as well as the balmy turquoise waters of the Caribbean Sea which gently lap its palm-fringed white sand beaches.

Located 19 kilometres or 12 miles off the coast of Quintana Roo, Cozumel is an island covered with lush jungle and surrounded by a rocky coastline, beaches, lagoons and mangroves. The waters encircling the island boast an impressive group of coral reefs which are part of the Great Mayan Reef, and they are home to an impressive diversity of marine life. Its only settlement is San Miguel de Cozumel, which has a relaxed Caribbean atmosphere. Back on the mainland, south of Cancun, Playa del Carmen, has been described as one of the most attractive beach destinations in the country. It's located in the heart of the Mayan Riviera, and a haven for lovers of the water sports, from snorkelling and windsurfing to kitesurfing, which is a new extreme sport combining surfing and parasailing. Lovers of diving can also access the Great Mayan Reef easily from Playa del Carmen, diving at depths of more than 10 metres or 33 feet, among tropical fish and coral which has existed for more than 500 years.

A MAN, A PLAN, A CANAL

Completed in 1914, the Panama Canal is the product of 35 years of sweat, tears, and the loss of 20,000 human lives. The 80-kilometre-long waterway connects the Atlantic and Pacific Oceans at the Isthmus of Panama. It cuts through the heart of what was once one of the earth's deadliest jungles, allowing ships of all kinds and sizes to glide effortlessly over the spine of an entire continent 26 metres or 85 feet above sea level. The convenience of cutting across a continent comes at a cost though; the price for a vessel to make a transit of the Canal depends on its size. In May 2008 the *Disney Magic*, a cruise ship which stretches an impressive 295-metres long, paid a record US $331,200 to make the crossing. But it wasn't always that expensive. In 1928, Richard Halliburton paid a mere 36 cents in tolls to swim the Canal in a journey which took 10 days as opposed to the eight hours it takes most ships today.

At one time, a transit of the Panama Canal was considered a once-in-a-lifetime opportunity. Today, however, more and more cruise passengers are repeating the journey, both for the Canal itself, which never fails to enthrall, and for the diverse ports of call in the two great oceans on either side. For those who love history, engineering marvels and cruising, it really can't be beaten. A typical transit begins at Gatun Locks on the Atlantic side of the Canal. After entering a lock, a ship is hooked up to locomotive 'mules' which will guide it into position, then the 700-ton behemoth gates close, and millions of gallons of fresh water being pouring into the chamber to lift the vessel to the level of the next lock. After passing through the Gatun Lock, ships drop into into Gatun Lake, a parking lot for all manner of cargo ships, freighters and other vessels waiting their turn to navigate the narrow Galliard Cut en route to the Pacific Ocean. And at the other end, three more locks wait to lower vessels back down to sea level.

In 2007 a multi-billion-dollar expansion plan got underway to build an additional set of locks to increase traffic, but it will take an estimated seven or eight years to complete the works. In the meantime, ships fight for transit slots in what has become an increasingly congested waterway. For a ship's captain, a transit through the Panama Canal is a stressful event, but for passengers it's a fascinating and leisurely experience that truly grips the imagination. All you have to do is sit back in a comfy chair, order a cool drink, and watch as one of the great engineering achievements of the 20th century passes right before your eyes.

FABULOUS FLORIDA

There are three destinations in Southern Florida which often appear in Caribbean cruise itineraries: Miami, Fort Lauderdale and Key West. Miami has been dubbed the 'cruise capital of the world' and for good reason; it's home to no less than eight major cruise lines, and is a major destination in its own right as well as the main starting point for many Caribbean cruises today. Aside from an impressive line-up of cruise ships and five-star resorts, one of the main attractions which keeps visitors returning is Miami Beach, an impressive man-made playground, which is also the home of the chic and historic Art Deco district on South Beach. SoBe, as the locals call it, sits on the south-west corner of Miami Beach, and even though it may be kitschy to some, this bright collection of pastel-coloured Pre-Depression buildings has a unique charm all of its own. It's one of the largest areas on the US National Register of Historic Places, and that's thanks to active local groups who've fought hard to prevent developers from bulldozing the 1920s built structures, and replacing them with the concrete and glass towers that proliferate on the far northern end of Miami Beach.

It's an area where retro is the main theme, from Marilyn Monroe statues to locals driving vintage cars, this is where it's possible to feel transported back in time.

Challenging Miami for its cruise crown, however, is neighbouring Fort Lauderdale. Called the 'Venice of America' because of its expansive network of canals, it is a popular yachting centre and also boasts a

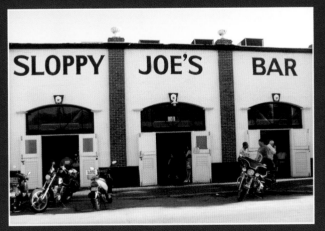

major cruise terminal which is also the jumping off point for many a Caribbean cruise. Among its other attractions are a long stretch of pristine beach which runs for 11 kilometres or seven miles, and a more laid-back genteel atmosphere without the crowds. Finally, there's Key West, the last in the chain of Florida's 'keys' with a reputation as a hangout for writers, artists, presidents and drop-outs. Attractions here include Hemingway's home, complete with its famous six-toed cats, and his favourite watering hole, Sloppy Joe's Bar. Another landmark is the southernmost point, which is closer to Havana than Miami by some 100 km (62 miles).

LEFT & RIGHT: The Caribbean is a natural playground

The Caribbean

It is easy to understand why the Caribbean archipelago is one of the world's top picks for a cruise vacation. Its warm, turquoise waters are home to a smorgasbord of landscapes and exotic islands, each with its own distinctive blend of culture, natural wonders, and laid-back charm. It's a stunning region boasting movie-set beauty: coconut-tree-clad mountains, verdant valleys of sugar cane and bananas, towering volcanoes, and coral reef teeming with colourful marine life. And when it comes to sun-drenched beaches, it has no shortage of picturesque locations to offer travellers seeking some fun in the sun. The Caribbean takes its name from the Carib, an ethnic group who occupied parts of the Lesser Antilles and adjacent areas of South America. It is also commonly called the West Indies, a throwback to the days of Christopher Columbus, who landed in the region in 1492 believing that he was in the Indies of Asia. The region is divided into two primary areas. To the north, there is the Greater Antilles, which includes the cluster of islands known as the Caymans, and the four larger islands of Cuba, Jamaica, Hispaniola and Puerto Rico. The other area is called the Lesser Antilles, which includes the smaller islands of the south and east.

THE GREATER ANTILLES

Made up of three islands, Grand Cayman, Little Cayman and Cayman Brac, the Cayman Islands iare a British Crown colony which boasts the highest standard of living in the Caribbean, thanks largely to the influence of the offshore banking industry. Until the 1970s the Cayman Islands were a sleepy British outpost in the western Caribbean, but in recent years the population has grown and the economy has taken off in a big way. It's now the fifth largest financial centre in the world, boasting more than 600 banks with assets in excess of $500 billion. Grand Cayman receives 95 per cent of the tourist traffic, and its allure extends beyond the banking sector. It's one of the world's best scuba diving areas because of its crystal-clear waters and pristine marine walls, and there are several sites where visitors can get up-close-and-personal with local marine wildlife. One of the most famous is Stingray City, described as 'the best 12 foot dive in the world'. Situated on North Sound, this is an experience which is unique and allows divers and snorkellers swim with with stingrays. Grand Cayman is also home of the famous Seven Mile Beach, a dazzling stretch of palm fringed white sand surrounded by crystal clear, aqua blue ocean, where it's possible to see colourful fish darting around in the water right up to the edge of the beach. Another popular tourist attraction is Hell, a bizarre group of short, black, limestone formations about half the size of a soccer field.

Puerto Rico is fondly called 'La Isla del Encanto' by its inhabitants, which translates to 'The Island of Enchantment'. But it's also a major hub in the world of Caribbean cruising, as well as in the Greater Antilles. A self-governing unincorporated territory of the United States since 1953, Puerto Rico is composed of a mini-archipelago which includes the main island of Puerto Rico, and a number of smaller islands and keys. Thanks to history, its modern heritage is clearly Spanish, but if you scratch beneath the surface you will discover that the roots of its culture are an exotic mix of African, indigenous Taíno, Spanish and, more recently, North American. The capital of Puerto Rico is San Juan, a unique walled city which was founded in 1521 and boasts one of the largest natural harbours in the Caribbean. It's also the second oldest city in the Americas after Santo Domingo. There are many sights to see in Puerto Rico, but top of the list is Old San Juan, a sub-city with cobblestone streets made from blue stone, more than 400 carefully restored 16th and 17th century Spanish colonial buildings, and a network of bustling plazas. There's also the six-level fortress El Morro, which towers 140 feet above sea level, the Catedral de San Juan, La Fortaleza, and Castillo de San Cristóbal, which played a major role in the city's defence.

For decades, travellers have regarded Jamaica as one of the most alluring of the Caribbean islands. The third largest island in the archipelago, it's a place that conjures up a variety of contrasting images: white sanded beaches, waterfalls, reggae artists, cricket, and the little known Blue Mountain Range. Three of the most visited cities in Jamaica include Montego Bay, Ocho Rios, and Negril, with each having their own charms and sights to see. Montego Bay is the second largest city on the island, a hub of shopping and restaurants boasting a backdrop of picturesque mountains. In contrast, Negril is one of the island's newest resort destinations, a sleepy enclave with a colourful heritage which was discovered in the 1700s by rowdy pirates. In the 1960s and 1970s, it was invaded by hippies from North America, but today its major drawcard is 11-kilometre-long (seven mile) beach, and spectacular sunsets thanks to its western location. Jamaica's cruise capital is Ocho Rios, a picturesque bay sheltered by lush, garden-like mountains and protected by coral reef. It's home to the famous Dunns River Falls, one of the most photographed and visited waterfalls in the world, which cascades from 182 metres or 600 feet above onto a beach.

CARIBBEAN CUISINE

Ask anyone to define the essence of Caribbean cuisine, and in many cases their answer will largely depend on which of the islands they have visited. In fact, thanks to its history, Caribbean cuisine can be compared to a cultural patchwork quilt. Just as its heritage is a complex fusion of nationalities, its cuisine is a smorgasbord of ethnic flavours, combined with local specialities which vary from island to island. The Arawak, Carib and Taíno Indians were the first inhabitants of the Caribbean Islands, and their daily diet is said to have consisted of vegetables and fruits such as papaw, yams, guavas, and cassava. The Taíno started the process of cooking meat and fish in large clay pots, while the Carib Indians added more spice to their food with hot pepper sauces. Then the Caribbean became a crossroads for the world, with the arrival of the Europeans and the African slaves they brought with them.

As in many cultures, food plays a central role in family life and the traditions of the Caribbean islands, and its diversity is quite extraordinary. There are many unique local ingredients used in cooking. They include ackee, a reddish-yellow fruit of an evergreen tree found in Jamaica, Boniato, a semi-sweet potato, chayote, a green, pear-shaped fruit used as a vegetable in salads or cooked, jicama, a root vegetable with a white, sweet, crisp flesh, and soursop, a dark green heart shaped fruit covered with soft spines. Common foods and dishes you will find travelling the islands include ceviche, seafood cooked with the acids of citrus juices and seasoned with herbs, chutney made from tropical fruits, escabeche, seafood that has been pan fried or poached then marinated in citrus of vinegar, pick-a-peppa sauce, which is a mango-tamarind based spicy sauce from Jamaica, and ropa vieja, which is shredded beef in a spicy sauce.

Although seafood is one of the most common cuisine types in the islands, each island has its own specialties; Barbados, for example, is famous for flying fish, while Trinidad and Tobago are known for crab. But 'jerk' or 'jerky' is also popular. The name actually refers to the process of rubbing spices and hot peppers onto strips of meat to tenderise and preserve them, but in Jamaica, Trinidad, Tobago and Barbados, an entire culinary art has grown up around them. As a result, there are many jerk seasoning combinations in the islands, and they are typically used on chicken or pork.

ABOVE: The *Seven Sea's Navigator* in St. Lucia

THE LESSER ANTILLES

The other 'half' of the Caribbean is made up of a long chain of islands, most of which wrap around the eastern end of the Caribbean Sea. They can be sub-divided into two main groups, the Windward Islands in the south, and the Leeward islands in the north. A third group is called the Leeward Antilles, found just north of Venezuela. The terms 'leeward' and 'windward' refer to islands in an archipelago and their different sides. The leeward side of an island is protected by the elevation of a prevailing wind, and typically are drier and less windy. In contrast, the windward side is subject to the prevailing wind. In the Caribbean, the prevailing winds blow from south to north, which means the southern islands are affected by wind first.

There are eight primary islands in the Windward Chain, including Martinique, St. Lucia, Barbados, Grenada and Trinidad. Discovered by Christopher Columbus in 1502, Martinique is one of the more refined of the larger islands. It's a genuine slice of France nestling in the tropics, where the islanders eat croissants and wear Paris fashions. The island is dominated by towering Mount Pelee, which last erupted in 1902, and while the southern half of the island is where you'll find all the beaches, the northern half is covered in lush rainforest. In contrast, Barbados has long been dubbed the 'Little England' of the Caribbean because of its long association as a British colony, the official language here is also English. The island's two sides are quite different. The eastern side stretches along rugged Atlantic coast, and is home to a popular surfing spot known as the 'Soup Bowl', while the western side of the island is quieter and more calm with tranquil bays. In its past, St. Lucia was juggled between French and British control, so often that is called 'Helen of the West Indies', likened to the mythical Helen of Troy. More mountainous than any of the other Caribbean islands, its highest point is Mount Gimie, which towers 950 metres or 3,120 feet above sea level.

Some of the better known of the Leeward Islands include the US Virgin Islands, Saint Martin, and Antigua. Although it's an unincorporated organized territory of the United States, the US Virgin Islands used to be known as the Danish West Indies. The three primary islands include St. Croix, Saint John and Saint Thomas, with the latter being the most popular when it comes to cruise itineraries, thanks to two main draw cards: duty free shopping and a picturesque spot called Magen's Bay. Directly across from the island's capital, Charlotte Amalie is a crescent-shaped bay boasting almost two kilometres of white sand and a small cluster of bars. Saint Martin is an unusual island of two halves split between the French and the Dutch, and it's one of the smallest land masses in the world shared between two countries.

The French half, Saint Martin, occupies the north of the island and 52 square kilometres or 20 square miles, while the southern side, which is about half the size, is Dutch. Look for the border on this island, however, and you will be hard-pressed to find it; the only giveaway that you've crossed from one 'side' to the other are the monuments and signs. Antigua, which until 1981 was British, is a famous getaway, and island paradise, for the rich and famous, known for scuba diving, sailing and five-star resorts.

Of the Netherlands Antilles, Bonaire and Curacao will be the most familiar. Until the abolition of slavery in 1863, Curaçao was once the centre of the Caribbean slave trade. And although its heritage is Dutch, the islanders have developed their own culture, and even a language of their own called Papiamentu, which is a native Creole.

PREVIOUS PAGE
Antigua

LEFT: *Crystal Symphony* cruises into St. Thomas

THE CARIBBEAN ABOVE THE WATER LINE

The balmy waters surrounding the Caribbean Islands are home to many amazing, exotic and colourful fish and sea creatures. They include hog fish, queen trigger fish, barracuda, marlin, bottlenose and spinner dolphins, moray eels, and several species of sea turtle including the loggerhead, leatherback and green. But not all of the action takes place in the water, or beneath its surface around the spectacular coral reefs. Ecologically, the Caribbean is classified as a neo-tropical zone, which means its vegetation is typical of the 'new world'. It has exceptional bird life, lizards, frogs, tapir, peccaries, ocelots and a host of other critters. When it comes to insects, however, aside from the pesky mosquito there are a number of exotic species which exist on the islands including tarantulas, scorpions, centipedes, dragonflies, leaf cutting ants, and click beetles. But one species which few people realise exist in abundance among the Caribbean islands is the butterfly.

There are several ways to see the butterflies of the islands, the primary one being to hike in the forests and countryside. But an easy way to really get up close and personal with hundreds of the species at once is by visiting one of the Caribbean butterfly farms. There are currently four; St. Martin, St. Thomas, Aruba and Grand Cayman. We had the opportunity of visiting the one in Grand Cayman, and it was a unique experience. The farm consists of a large meshed structure which contains a beautifully landscaped garden filled with exotic flowers, trees, fountains, and pools with Japanese fish. The atmosphere is tranquil, and thousands of brightly coloured butterflies fly freely, and safely, around. It pays to wear colourful clothing and perfume when you visit, as the butterflies are attracted to colour and the sweet smell, and will often land on you out of curiosity.

Aside from being a tourist attraction, however, the Caribbean butterfly farms are also there to promote a strong environmental message. These beautiful creatures are not as abundant as they once were, with many species now endangered. As a result, the farms are helping to protect and conserve the butterflies so that they can remain a part of the eco-system as well as be of joy to humans.

LEFT: Champagne sunset

Today, Curaçao is a popular tourist destination which has many curiosities, one of which is the architecture in its capital city, Willemstad. Reminiscent of a Dutch town, the buildings have bright red roofs and painted in bright, pastel colours. The city is also divided into two halves by a major canal, with Punda on one side and Otrobanda on the other. The pair are linked by a famous moving foot bridge called the Queen Emma Brug. In contrast, the island of Bonaire is a flat with little vegetation except for sandy beaches and salt hills, but its famous for some spectacular dive spots.

CUISINE AT SEA, THE VINTAGE ROOM

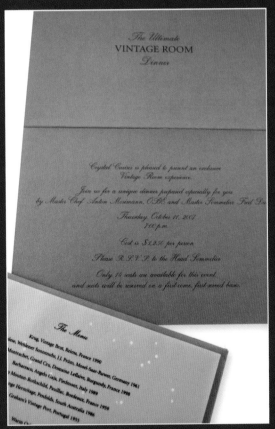

With fine dining now an important and integral part of the cruise experience, Crystal Cruises upped the ante a few years ago with the creation of an additional dining venue on its two ships, the *Crystal Serenity* and the *Crystal Symphony*. Called The Vintage Room, it's an elite private dining room accommodating 12-14 guests, and is designed to appeal to a discriminating palate, as well as promote wine appreciation. Guests wishing to hold a private party can reserve the dining room during their cruise. They can choose from an array of fine wines from an exclusive reserve list, and once the wines have been selected, the ship's executive chef then creates a special menu to complement the wines chosen.

Several times a year, however, this elegant and exclusive space is opened up for an 'Ultimate Vintage Room Dinner', a one-of-a-kind gastronomic experience featuring some of the rarest wines in the world. These feasts are held only a few times a year on both of its ships and are clearly aimed at true connoisseurs, and they cost in excess of US$1000 per head. The first event held was an extravagant eight-course French dinner prepared by Master Chef André Soltner, the former chef/owner of world-famous *Lutèce*. It was paired with, among others, a nearly impossible-to-get 1959 Château Lafite - Rothschild, Pauillac, Bordeaux and a Screaming Eagle 1996 from Napa Valley, considered its dream year. These special dining events draw the world's top chefs, including Anton Mosimann on a cruise from Istanbul to Athens in 2007, and Piero Selvaggio of the famed Valentino restaurants on a cruise from Beijing to Hong Kong in 2008.

Cocktails

Tequila Sunrise

2 parts tequila
1 part Grenadine
1 part fresh lemon juice
soda water
a slice of lime

Shake all of the ingredients together in a cocktail shaker with ice,
strain into a highball glass, garnish with the lime and serve.

Pink Daiquiri

2 parts Bacardi Rum
2-3 dashes of Grenadine
½ part of fresh lime juice

Add all ingredients to a cocktail shaker filled with ice,
strain into a chilled martini glass and serve.

RIGHT: Pink Daiquiri

Recipes

Marinated Caribbean Pineapple with Sorbet

2 small pineapples
1 cup pineapple juice
½ cup Bacardi rum
1 cup plus 3 tbsp sugar
2 tbsp fresh lemon juice
fresh mint, coarsely chopped

Peel and core one of the of the pineapples, slice very thinly, and arrange the slices on a platter. In a jug, mix the rum, 1 tablespoon of sugar and the pineapple juice, and pour over the pineapple to marinate. Refrigerate for 2–3 hours.

To make the sorbet, peel and core the other pineapple, and cut into 5cm (2in) pieces. Place in a food processor with the lemon juice and mix until smooth. Then add the sugar and continue mixing for about one minute, or until the sugar dissolves. Pour the mixture into a container and freeze for around 1–2 hours. To serve, remove the pineapple slices from the marinade and arrange on a platter. Sprinkle with the chopped mint, and add a few scoops of the sorbet on top.

Serves 8

Red Snapper with Fresh Salsa

(Supplied by chef Anton Mosimann)

4 red snapper fillets of around 150g (5oz) each
5 tsp olive oil
paprika

Salsa
2 large, ripe tomatoes, skinned and seeded
1 medium red onion, peeled
1 green capsicum, seeded
1–2 fresh green chillies, seeded
2 garlic cloves, peeled
1 tbsp red wine vinegar
2 tbsp finely chopped fresh coriander
salt and freshly ground pepper

To make the salsa, finely dice the tomatoes, onion, green pepper, chillies and garlic, and combine in a large glass bowl. Add the red wine vinegar and coriander, and season to taste with salt and pepper. Cover and chill for up to 6 hours, stirring occasionally.

Preheat a grill to high, then spread a little of the salsa over a foil-lined grill pan and place the fish fillets, skin side up, on top in one layer. Brush the fish with the olive oil and season to taste with paprika, salt and pepper, then grill for about six minutes or until the fish is cooked. There is no need to turn the fillets over. Serve the hot fish on a platter with the remaining cold salsa.

Serves four

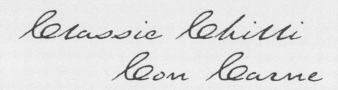

Classic Chilli Con Carne

700g (1.5lb) lean minced beef
2 large onions
6 garlic gloves, minced
2 x 400g (14oz) tins of chopped tomatoes
2 green capsicums, diced
4 red chillies, finely chopped
1 400g (14oz) tin of red kidney beans
Tabasco sauce
Worcestershire sauce
1 tbsp barbecue sauce
1 tbsp sour cream
1 tbsp olive oil
½ cup beef stock
2 cups of white rice, uncooked
1 iceberg lettuce, finely chopped
6 large, ripe tomatoes, diced
1 cup of hard cheese, grated
1 large bag of plain corn chips

Heat the olive oil and a little of the stock in a deep frying pan or large saucepan, and cook the onions, garlic, chillies and capsicum for a few minutes until soft. Add the meat and cook for about five or six minutes until it changes colour. Then add the tomatoes, the barbecue sauce, the remaining stock, and a good shake of Worcestershire sauce. Cover and cook for about one hour, until the liquid is reduced to a thick sauce.

To prepare the accompaniments, cook or steam the rice, and arrange a serving platter with the chopped lettuce, tomatoes and the grated cheese. About ten minutes prior to serving the chilli, add the kidney beans, the sour cream, and a few drops of Tabasco sauce to the meat. To serve, put a serving of rice and chilli into a bowl, and garnish with 2–3 corn chips.

Serves six

Chicken Quesadilla

2 large chicken breasts, skin off
8 tortillas
2 large, ripe avocados
1 punnet cherry tomatoes, diced
1 large can of sweet corn, drained
3 cups of hard cheese, grated
jalapeño chillies, finely chopped (optional)
Tabasco sauce

Slice the chicken, stir-fry in a little olive oil and set aside. Then cut the
avocados in half, and divide the flesh between four of the tortillas, spreading
thinly. Then, working in layers, add the tomatoes and a sprinkle of sweet
corn, followed by the chicken pieces, and finally a few drops of Tabasco
sauce. Add the chillies if desired, and finish off by adding the cheese. To
cook, you can use a sandwich maker, an electric grill or an electric fry pan.
Cook for approximately three minutes on each side (if you have to turn over)
or until the cheese is melted and the tortilla is browned. To serve, cut each
tortilla into four segments.

Serves four

The Cruise Lines

Regent Seven Seas Cruises

Over the past decade, Regent has established itself as a leader at the luxury end of the cruise market. It currently operates four luxury ships which circumnavigate the globe year-round, boasting some of the highest space-to-passenger ratios of any cruise line afloat. Exceptional service, exciting itineraries, and some amazing on-board facilities keep well-travelled guests returning. They include spacious, luxurious accommodations, open seating fine dining, enrichment programs featuring expert lecturers, famous guest chefs, and Carita of Paris spas. Other attractions include alternative dining venues, including the Le Cordon Bleu restaurants, Signatures, which feature on two of its ships. Each year, Regent also offers one of the most comprehensive world cruises available in cruising today, and in 2009, this innovative cruise line raised the bar again by offering two.

Regent's luxury fleet currently comprises three mid-sized ships—the *Seven Seas Navigator* (490 guests), the *Seven Seas Voyager* (700 guests), and the Seven Seas Mariner (700 guests)—and the more intimate *Paul Gauguin* (330 guests), which is permanently based in Tahiti.

When it comes to awards and accolades, Regent has a growing list to its name. The *Seven Seas Mariner* holds pride of position for being the first all-suite, all-balcony cruise ship to take to the high seas, and her sister ship, the *Seven Seas Voyager*, is the second. Regent won 'Best Small Ship Cruise Line' in the esteemed *Condé Nast Traveler* Readers' Choice Awards in 2007, and 'Best For Rooms' and 'Best For Design' in the *Condé Nast Traveler* Gold List in 2008. In 2008, the *Paul Gauguin* won the 'Highest-Ranked Small Luxury Cruise Ship' in *Condé Nast Traveler's* Readers' Poll. Regent's other three ships earned a 'Six Plus Stars Rating' in Stern's Guide to the Cruise Vacation in 2008.

Regent Seven Seas Cruises is based in Fort Lauderdale, Florida. For more information, visit www.rssc.com.

Crystal Cruises

Since launching in 1988, Crystal Cruises has taken its philosophy of the 'Crystal Difference' around the globe, and today it is regarded as one of the top cruise lines in the world. It currently operates two large-size luxury ships, both of which offer discerning travellers the kind of luxury at sea which you expect from the world's finest land-based hotels. The 'Crystal Difference' is all about quality, attention to detail, exceptional service and choices. On board attractions which keep its loyal guests returning for more include fine dining, creative pursuits at sea, themed cruises, alternative dining venues, and award winning spas and leisure facilities. Both ships also boast the only restaurants at sea operated by the legendary Japanese chef, Nobu Matsuhisa—Silk Road and the Sushi Bar. Each year, Crystal ships follow varied itineraries which take guests to the most important cruise regions in the globe. In 2009, a 106-day world cruise was offered which included visits to 17 countries along the Pacific Rim.

Crystal operates two large-size ships, the *Crystal Symphony* (940 guests) and the *Crystal Serenity* (1092 guests). On the *Crystal Symphony*, 57 per cent of the staterooms have private balconies, on the *Crystal Serenity*, 85 per cent. Crystal also has a growing list of awards and accolades to its name. The *Crystal Serenity* won first place for 'Best Cruise Ships In The World' (medium-sized category) in *Condé Nast Traveler's* Readers' Choice Awards in 2008, while the *Crystal Symphony* was second. Both ships have also won numerous awards in *Condé Nast Traveler's* Gold List between 1997 and 2008.

Crystal Cruises is based in Los Angeles, California. For more information, visit www.crystalcruises.com.

Cocktails

Cuisine

Destinations

03. Western Mediterranean

04. Asia

07. Mexico & The Caribbean

First published in Australia in 2009 by
New Holland Publishers (Australia) Pty Ltd
Sydney • Auckland • London • Cape Town

1/66 Gibbes Street Chatswood NSW 2067 Australia
218 Lake Road Northcote Auckland New Zealand
86 Edgware Road London W2 2EA United Kingdom
80 McKenzie Street Cape Town 8001 South Africa

Copyright © 2009 New Holland Publishers (Australia) Pty Ltd
Copyright © 2009 in text Joanna and Ben Hall
Copyright © 2009 in photographs Ben Hall, unless otherwise credited

All rights reserved. No part of this publication may be reproduced, stored in a retrieval system
or transmitted, in any form or by any means, electronic, mechanical, photocopying, recording
or otherwise, without the prior written permission of the publishers and copyright holders.

A record of this book is held at the National Library of Australia

ISBN 9781741106534

Publisher: Fiona Schultz
Publishing Manager: Lliane Clarke
Junior Editor: Ashlea Wallington
Senior Editor: Joanna Tovia
Designer: Hayley Norman
Production Manager: Olga Dementiev
Printer: SNP/Leefung Printing Co. Ltd (China)
10 9 8 7 6 5 4 3 2 1